D1520122

KETOGENIC DIET: 30 DAY KETOGENIC CHALLENGE

Ketogenic Diet

30 Day Ketogenic Challenge

Discover the Secret to Health and Rapid Weight Loss with the Ketogenic 30 Day Challenge; Ketogenic Cookbook with Complete 30 Day Meal Plan

By: Marie Amherst

Legal notice

Want MORE healthy recipes for FREE?

Double down on healthy living with a full week of fresh, healthy salad recipes. A new salad for every day of the week!

Grab this bonus recipe ebook *free* as our gift to you:

http://salad7.hotbooks.org

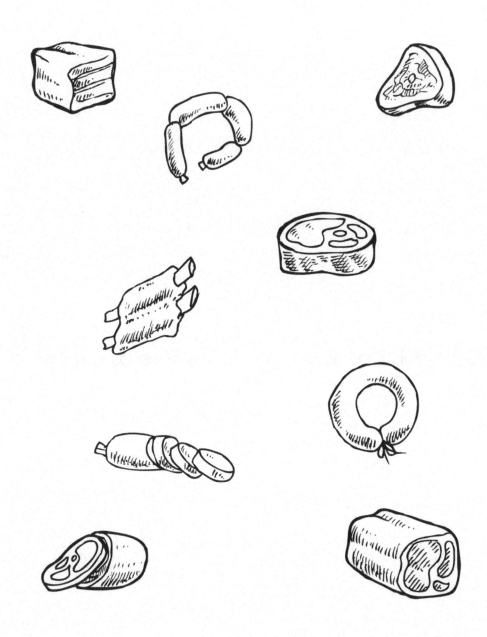

Contents

What is the Keto Diet?

When it comes to fueling up, you want to ensure that you're using the appropriate fuel. This applies to cars, but it really applies to our bodies as well. In America, many people are using processed and packaged foods to fuel themselves. But these foods are actually less efficient for our bodies. Even I did this for a large portion of my life.

The Ketogenic Diet Journey

When I was 16, I was in the library. I tried on a friend's coat when I heard a boy yell about a fat girl in a small coat. This was the moment that I wanted to change.

When I was working on getting in shape then, I cut down on the amount of fat that I was eating. I worked out constantly. However, this series of actions left me still fat and even more frustrated. Once I reached that point, I worked on focusing on nutrition. I was going to struggle for a while with everything that I had been taught throughout the years, but I would eventually get over. The most frightening prospect was eating real fat.

Adding fat to my diet did have some great benefits. I was sleeping more soundly, feeling calmer, and feeling so much better in that very first week than I ever had. There are biochemical reasons that restricting fat isn't the way to really boost your health. Good tasting foods are often thought to be unhealthy for you, but that's not necessarily true. You can have delicious food and feel better too.

You don't have to deprive yourself of delicious foods like cheesecake, cheese, butter, and avocados. All of that can be part of your diet as long as it is nutrient dense. You may even lose a good amount of weight while on this date.

Getting into losing weight is a difficult job. But once you find the right foods for the job, you'll find that weight loss will come more quickly and more easily than ever before. By using knowledge about hormones like leptin and insulin along with the diet that I was working on, I managed to realign my hormones and get rid of some food cravings.

And the best part of my diet was that I didn't have to deprive myself as much as I thought was going to have to. Instead, the diet was going to let me have some interesting foods added to my diet that were going to make everything more rounded out and delicious. It was something I never imagined happening in my life time.

What is the Ketogenic Diet?

On the most basic level, this diet is low in carbs, moderate with proteins, and high in fats. This combination will have amazing benefits to your health. This particular diet was created in 1921 at the Mayo Clinic in Minnesota. It was specifically for patients that were struggling with seizures. After anti-seizure medication hit the market, the diet was forgotten for quite a while. It was in 1994 that the diet came back around being mentioned in an episode of Dateline NBC. It was used by Jim Abrahams, a film director, to treat his son's seizures.

Because his son, Charlie, wasn't responding to the medication, they had turned to the diet. After starting the ketogenic diet, Charlie was eventually seizure-free. The Abrahams started a foundation, The Charlie Foundation, in order to raise awareness about the diet when people need it to deal with epilepsy.

After that time, there has been more and more attention on the diet. This has led to realizations that the diet can help with cognition, body composition, inflammation reduction, and hormone regulation, as well as much more.

With this diet, you will be able to really feel better, sleep better, and get your hormones in check. These foods will keep you feeling full and satisfied while you're working on your body goals. You won't have to miss out on desserts and other things during this diet. You're going to hear more and more about the benefits that the ketogenic diet. There is more and more research that is being led on the subject of true ketogenic diets.

There are some diets that are advertised as ketogenic but are not truly in that category. Just because it is low-carb doesn't mean that it's ketogenic. The RDA recommends that you have 300 grams of carbs every day. Just because a diet has 150 grams of carbs included in the daily allotment does not make the diet low-carb or ketogenic. Some of these diets don't contain enough of the right nutrients or contain too much of others. A true ketogenic diet is structured in a particular way. And some diets used in studies don't allow for the subject to reach ketosis. Some people are able to reach ketosis during that time period, but there are many more people that cannot reach it in that time frame.

What is not in a ketogenic diet?
The ketogenic diet isn't just about protein.

If you eat too much protein, your body will turn the protein into sugar through a process of gluconeogenesis. Eating too much protein would be as bad as eating a ton of carbs.

The ketogenic diet isn't just about eliminating sugars.

The diet is about reducing the amount of carbs in your diet. But even a low-carb diet needs a little bit of clarification. We know that sugar is bad for us, but not a lot of people understand how foods turn into sugars. Grains, starchy vegetables, and fruits are the typical foods that turn into sugars.

While I might be more flexible with my own diet, I've found that some people need to be stricter with their ketogenic diets. Starch in any form was too much for some of the clients that I worked with. Our ancestors ate plenty of starchy vegetables, but their metabolisms were built for that kind of food.

But our modern diets are filled with dyes, fructose, pesticides, MSG, and many other chemicals. Because of the kind of stuff that we're putting into our bodies, we have to have a much stricter approach because of how damaged the cells are.

There are people out there that can have sweet potatoes and fruits while on this kind of diet, but that doesn't mean that they are actually healthy. In fact, some people that include sweet potatoes and fruits had extremely high blood sugar. Because of the way that we have been treating our bodies, we have to be stricter with the diet. It may be simple in theory, but you'll find that there's some trouble in actually executing the job.

Inflammation, Sugar, and Insulin

In order to start talking about the ways that insulin, weight gain, and inflammation work together. This means talking about what exactly we are consuming. Eating too many carbs or too much protein will mean that your blood sugar levels are going to stay higher longer. When there's too much glucose in the bloodstream, you'll find that it's just like having tar in your bloodstream. It can cause serious problems such as increasing any risk for coronary artery diseases.

After that, the sugars and starches get turned into fat and stored in the body. The muscles in the body have a layer on them called the glycation. These cells won't take glycogen from the bloodstream. As well, your insulin will stop your body from producing lipase. The enzyme allows your body to metabolize stored fat.

If you're consuming foods like oatmeal before you're working out, then you won't be able to burn fat in the way that you want. You will continue to be insulin resistant and only burn sugar.

This information might sound bad, but there's unfortunately more. When your body is insulin-resistant, then your pancreas will kick into overdrive and create more insulin. This can destroy your body. It can cause cancer, buildup in the arteries, as well as damage on the cellular levels. Some people even experience nerve damage from excess insulin in their bodies.

In addition to the excess insulin, starch and sugar can also cause damage to the nerve tissue. Our typical breakfasts cannot only cause our bodies from becoming insulin resistant, but the covering over the cells can block the essential amino acids from entering into the cells as well. These amino acids are essential for the body's ability to create proteins. If your body can't get a hold on some amino acids, it will then turn to your muscles to be able to make proteins. This cannibalistic nature happens when the body thinks that there are not enough sugars in the cells.

With all that information in mind, what do you need to know? Well, if your body is insulin resistant, you may start having thyroid issues. It happens because your liver is unable to convert the hormone T4 into T3. This will make you feel tired and crave more carbs. You'll be low energy and less feel like you can't exercise

Inflammation and Sugar

People sometimes tell me that they're on a diet that is low-sugar and anti-inflammatory, but they might not actually be. Replacing table sugar with fruits doesn't necessarily reduce inflammation. The fruits might be better for someone that has a healthy metabolism, but it doesn't always help everyone. Anti-inflammatory diets will cut out sugar in its entirety. This also means cutting starch. This is where a ketogenic diet can step in.

Sugar is constantly spoken about in commercials and health magazines. There's a reason why people are saying a lot of negative things about sugar. It is causing problems. However, these people that are criticizing sugar often turn around tell people to eat something like a banana when they're craving sugar. But the banana has sugar in it, which is why the craving goes away. Kombucha has sugar in it, too.

While kombucha and bananas aren't as bad as eating KitKat bars, but there is still sugar there. I'm not judging you for sometimes making these mistakes. I've made similar ones while I was on my journey to losing weight. At some point, I was eating dried prunes because I thought they were actually fat-free. I thought I was making the right choice, but I was fifty pounds over the weight that I wanted to be.

Let's take a look at a day of 'healthy' eating in my office. I have clients come in all the time that think that they are eating healthily. One client described her diet on her better days. On those days, she was having an egg-white omelet and chicken sausages for breakfast. She would have eighteen raw-vegan nut-flour crackers as a snack. During lunch, she would have sautéed turkey in a chicken brother. Her dinner typically consisted of low-starch vegetables. There are a couple reasons why this diet wasn't burning fat.

- There was too much protein in her diet, some of which was being turned into sugar.
- There wasn't any healthy fat in the diet.
- While she was listing her best days, she sometimes got cravings that led to her having many less than great days.

I understood quickly why her health wasn't where it was supposed to be.

Getting Rid of Sugar Intake and its Consequences

If you want to avoid all of the negative side effects of sugar, then we're going to go over how you can get around them. It will take some steps, but all of them are within your abilities.

You'll want to start by lowering the amount of carbohydrates that you are consuming, moderating the protein you are ingesting, and adding healthy fats to your diet. You'll want to also try to spread this diet to your friends and family, especially any children in your life. You don't want them to be insulin sensitive like we are.

You'll want to exercise. This isn't just about burning calories, but about helping your hormones balance themselves. This can be as simple as taking a walk after your meal. Your body will really be able to burn off the glycogen as fuel during that simple workout. There is a thought going around that you have to burn more calories than you're consuming in order to lose that weight. When you work out, you build muscle. Through the mitochondria in your new muscle cells, the fat will be oxidized. That is how you will be able to improve your body.

But those are the two main steps that you need to take. That's right, there are only two main steps that you need to take.

How to Adapt to Fat

When you're looking to get into a ketogenic diet, you're going to have to start by cutting out the sugars and starches. Those complex carbohydrates are glucose molecules, which means that they break down into just glucose, which is sugar. For a keto-adapted diet, you will need to be using ketones for energy instead.

The term ketones might be unfamiliar to you. Ketones are creating during the process of fat oxidation. They are a kind of super-fuel that your body really uses well. These are a great source of energy. Your liver is where they are created. The fatty acids are broken into acetyl-CoA. These are then oxidized and the energy created by that process is used to create ATP. This will carry energy to the cells.

After this process, if there is extra acetyl-CoA, then it will be turned into ketone bodies. This means that even when your body is creating ATP, you will be able to produce ketones at the same time. Your body will be a state of mild ketosis after a long night of sleep if you haven't eaten right before bed or right after you've woken up. This is roughly 10 hours. That is the amount of time that you will have to fast during to put your body into a mild ketosis.

If you want to start producing those ketones, then you might want to start by eating less than 10 grams of carbs in a single day. This may seem really hard at first, but there is a simple way to get into it. You will want to consume fatty meats as well as coconut oil to help fuel your body with the right kind of nutrients.

Entering a state of ketosis can also be started by increasing the amount of healthy fats that you are eating. This is in conjunction with reducing the amount of carbs that you are consuming. Your body will become used to turning the fat into energy and that will also translate to the fat on your body.

You will need to eat an amount of fat that relates to the caloric intake needs that you have. There is an equation for this: (total required calories*.8)/9=grams of fat. For example, if you were looking to have a caloric intake of 1,400 total calories, then you would need to consume 124 grams of fat to get the appropriate amount of calories from good fat that you needed.

Eating that much fat might be a little bit intimidating. However, you don't have to just eat fatty meat. You can add MCTs (medium-chain triglycerides) to what you eat in order to get that good fat. The oils from MCTs go straight to your liver to take part in the transformation that takes place there. In general, MCTs will help you increase the amount of ketone that you are creating.

MCTs are different than the related long-chain triglycerides. MCTs are absorbed quickly compared to the long-chain version. Because of how quickly they are used by the body, I am very specific with the recommendations that I make. I even get specific about the salad dressings that I suggest. When you can, you should be making your own dressings so that you can get MCTs instead vegetable oils. Vegetable oil is generally long-chain, which means that it's not going to become ketones or be as effective. MCT oils will not overwhelm your liver when it comes to creating ATP. Coconut oil and animal fats are great for this because they have a high concentration of MCT.

When you consume MCTs, you'll find that they are diffused through the gastrointestinal tract with the changes that are required for the long-chain acids. They are even easier on your body because they don't need bile salts when digested. Some patients that are suffering from malnutrition or have problems absorbing nutrients will find that MCTs are best. They work well with the body. However, even though MCTs are great, you should start slow. Adding too much too quickly to your diet can make you feel a little bit nauseous.

Proper Protein Intake

As we have covered, the ketogenic diet is about low-carb, high-fat, and moderate-protein intake. You don't want to have too much protein in your diet. This can become sugar as well. So when you're working on your body, you will want to make sure that you don't go overboard with the protein.

Knowing how much protein is too much is a tricky question. Everyone is a little bit different. There are some extreme cases where individuals can't have more than 60 grams of protein during the day. However, there is a rule of thumb that you can use. 0.7xyour lean body mass=grams of protein. If you weight 150 and have 25% body fat, then you have 105 pounds of lean mass. Once you input that number into the equation, you'll find out that you should have roughly 73.5 grams of protein.

- To summarize your journey to adapting to the ketogenic diet:
- Cut out the sugars and starches. You want to have less than 10 grams per day.
- Cut down your protein intake to 0.7 times your current lean body mass as grams of protein per day.
- Fill your diet with healthy fats that come from animals, avocados, and coconut.

How to Avoid the Common Side Effects of the Ketogenic Diet

When you start a low-carb diet, you may find that there are some unpleasant side effects that come around. I want to take a moment to tell you about the side effects and how you can best get around them. I like to think of my approach to the ketogenic as a way of minimizing the side effects and maximizing the benefits that come from the diet.

Quantity of Carbs

When you've heard about low-carb diets in the past, you have likely heard that they're not great and that they just don't work. However, the diets that are used in these studies aren't really truly low carb. They lower the carb intake to 150 grams of carbs per day. However, they don't get rid of gluten and often forget about dairy.

Lowering your diet from 300 grams of carbs to 150 grams might seem like a low-carb diet, but that isn't true. A ketogenic diet will get you closer to 30 grams of carbs per day. Getting rid of the complex carbs as well will make sure that your body will work harder at burning that fat.

Craving Sugar

When you get into a ketogenic diet, you will find that your desire for sugar and carbs will go away. However, getting to that point does take some time. You will want to completely avoid the carbs and sugars (even if you're only indulging in them on the weekends. When I have clients that are struggling with this, I suggest adding some supplements (liquid zinc, magnesium, 5-HTP, and bifido bacteria) to help curb those cravings before they get too bad.

Electrolytes and Sodium

People also experience headaches, dizziness, cramping, fatigue, and light headedness. These are symptoms that come on during the beginning of the diet. Not everyone will have these problems, but if you do find that you're feeling this way, then you're going to find that salt and minerals will be able to help you.

If there is a lot of insulin in your blood, then you'll find that this will have a lot of bad effects. It makes you store your energy as fat. This is just one of the ways that it can harm you. Some of these aren't visible. The worst side effect of excess insulin is that it will tell your kidneys to hold onto fluid. In some people, the effects of this water retention can be dramatic. Some people fluctuate with 20 pounds that come from water retention. This can cause pitting edema in the legs.

You can easily test if you have this by pressing your finger into the tissue of your shin bone. When you press, you might leave an indent there. This means that you are experiencing pitting edema. Obese clients that I have had experience this sensation in the afternoon or after they've been on their feet for long periods of time. The water retention gets to the lower legs and soaks into the soft tissue there.

This is shifted when you sleep and the water moves back up to your upper body. However, it comes back after another day on your feet. Some people experience this even if they aren't overweight, but people that are overweight will often find this is much more noticeable.

Adapting to the ketogenic lifestyle can cause people to rapidly improve when it comes to how sensitive they are to insulin. Your insulin levels will fall and the kidneys will release fluid. This can cause you to need to urinate a little more often. This goes away as you continue on the diet, but it is a little bit annoying.

The good news about releasing excess fluid is that the fat oxidation process is easier for your body. On the other hand, you may find that you have less sodium and electrolytes in your body. As your sodium levels drop, you may start feeling some of those side effects that we mentioned earlier.

Starting a low-carb lifestyle can cause you to feel faint, but don't chalk that up to your lack of sugar. This is because you are dehydrated. However, you will need water that has sodium in it to replenish your body. Add a little bit of salt to food, drink broth or even take sodium tablets. Salt isn't necessarily evil, especially when it isn't being consumed in excessive amounts from processed food.

Before You Begin Your Challenge

The ketogenic diet is emphatically *not* about starving yourself by eating tiny portions or worrying about every calorie. That is not how you lose weight with ketosis or how you live a healthy life. In fact, quite the opposite: it guarantees failure because you will likely be too miserable to complete the challenge.

If the recipe you are making yields four "servings" it does not mean you need to eat the meal with four other people. It also does not mean you need to eat only one serving yourself. Fortunately, that is *not* how keto works. Eat until you are satisfied, regardless of whether that means consuming one serving, or two, or ten. It is your *net carb consumption* that really matters when it comes to ketosis, but if you are following this meal plan then you don't really need to worry about that either. This meal plan is specifically designed to ensure as long as you are not gorging yourself at every single meal for a month, your diet will be sufficiently low in net carbs to achieve the state of ketosis.

Day 1:

Breakfast: Apple Crepes

Servings: 4

Calories: 411, Total Fat: 37 g, Saturated Fat: 9.3 g, Carbs: 6 g, Sugars: 1.2 g, Protein: 14 g

---

INGREDIENTS FOR THE BATTER:
4 large eggs
4 oz cream cheese
1/4 tsp sea salt
1/2 tsp baking soda

INGREDIENTS FOR THE TOPPINGS:
1 small gala apple, sliced thinly
2 oz chopped pecans, roasted
4 oz brie cheese, sliced
Fresh mint leaves, for garnish

To prepare the batter, add the ingredients to your blender and blend until smooth. Heat some oil in a frying pan on medium. Pour about ¼ cup of the batter into the pan, swirl it around to spread it evenly and fry until golden. Flip and fry on the other side as well. Transfer to a plate and repeat the same with the remaining batter.
To serve the crepes, top each with the apple slices, chopped pecans, and cheese. Fold, garnish with mint leaves and serve.

Lunch: Pesto Egg Muffins

Servings: 10 muffins

Calories: 125, Total Fat: 10.2 g, Saturated Fat: 3.5 g, Carbs: 1.9 g, Sugars: 0.5 g, Protein: 6.9 g

6 large eggs
3 tbsp pesto
Salt, to taste
Black pepper, to taste
⅔ cup frozen spinach, thawed and drained

¼ cup sun-dried tomatoes, chopped
4.5 oz soft goat cheese
½ cup kalamata olives, pitted and sliced

Preheat your oven to 350F / 176C.
Beat the eggs, add the pesto, season with salt and pepper and mix well to combine.
Fill the muffin cups with the spinach, tomatoes, cheese, and olives. Pour in the eggs to fill the cups and bake in the oven for about 25 minutes.
When baked, allow to cool for a few minutes and serve.

Dinner: Stuffed Avocado

Serves: 2

Calories: 550, Total Fat: 49 g, Saturated Fat: 11.6 g, Carbs: 14 g, Sugars: 0.8 g, Protein: 16 g

1 large ripe avocado, halved
2 cups chopped cauliflower, steamed
1 tbsp heavy cream
4 tbsp butter, melted
1/4 tsp onion powder

1/2 - 1 tsp sea salt
1/8 tsp black pepper
1/2 cup shredded cheddar
1 tsp chopped chives
1/2 cup crumbled bacon

Preheat your oven to 375F / 190C.
Scoop out the avocado meat into your blender. Add the cauliflower, cream, butter, onion powder, salt, and pepper. Blend until the mixture has become smooth and creamy.
Pour the mixture into the avocado shells, sprinkle with the cheddar cheese and bake in the preheated oven for 15-20 minutes.
When baked, garnish with the chives and bacon and serve.

Day 2:

Breakfast: Lemony Poppy Seed Pancakes

Servings: 4

Calories: 355, Total Fat: 26 g, Saturated Fat: 9.5 g, Carbs: 6.5 g, Sugars: 2.5 g, Protein: 23 g

INGREDIENTS FOR THE PANCAKES:
6 large eggs
25 drops liquid stevia
13 oz whole milk ricotta cheese
2 large lemons, zest and juice
1 1/2 tsp vanilla extract
1/2 cup almond flour
1 1/2 tsp baking powder

1 1/2 tbsp poppy seeds
1/4 tsp sea salt
INGREDIENTS FOR THE LEMON GLAZE:
1/2 lemon, juice and zest, divided use
1/2 cup powdered erythritol
1 splash almond mil

To prepare the pancakes:
Add the wet ingredients to your blender together with half the lemon juice and zest and blend until combined.
Add the dry ingredients and blend until combined into a smooth batter.
Heat some oil in a frying pan, pour in about ¼ cup of the batter and fry until bubbly and golden. Flip and cook for a minute or two until golden on the other side as well. Repeat the same with the remaining batter.
To prepare the lemon glaze:
Mix together the ingredients, pour them over the pancakes and serve.

Lunch: Bacon & Avocado Salad

Servings: 2

Calories: 337, Total Fat: 27 g, Saturated Fat: 12.1 g, Carbs: 7 g, Sugars: 0 g, Protein: 19 g

1 chicken breast, grilled, sliced

1 ripe avocado, sliced

1 cup crumbled bacon

Creamy Caesar dressing

Add the ingredients to a bowl, drizzle with the dressing and toss to combine.
Divide between two serving bowl and serve.

Dinner: Double Beef Stew

Servings: 4
Calories: 222, Total Fat: 7 g, Saturated Fat: 2.2 g, Carbs: 11 g, Sugars: 0.1 g, Protein: 27 g

30 oz diced tomatoes
1.5 lbs beef stew meet
1 cup beef broth
1 tbsp chili mix

1 tbsp Worcestershire sauce
2 tsp hot sauce
Salt, to taste

Add the ingredients to your crock pot. Set on high and cook for 6 hours.
Shred the meat, taste and adjust the seasonings.
Set on low and cook for 2 more hours. Serve warm.

Day 3:

Breakfast: Zucchini & Chicken Quiche

Servings: 10 slices

Calories: 311, Total Fat: 25 g, Saturated Fat: 7.4 g, Carbs: 4 g, Sugars: 2.0 g, Protein: 18 g

INGREDIENTS FOR THE CRUST:
2 cups almond flour
1 pinch sea salt
1 large egg
2 tbsp coconut oil
INGREDIENTS FOR THE FILLING:
Olive oil, for frying
1 lb ground chicken

6 large eggs
1 tsp dried oregano
1 tsp fennel seed
1 tsp salt
1/2 tsp black pepper
1/2 cup heavy cream
1-2 medium zucchini, grated

Preheat your oven to 350F / 176C. Grease a pie dish (approx. 9-inch dish) and set aside.

To prepare the crust:

Add the almond flour and salt to your blender or food processor and pulse a few times to combine. Add the egg and coconut oil and pulse until the mixture turns into a dough. Transfer to the prepared dish and press until distributed evenly.

To prepare the filling:

Heat some oil in a skillet, add the chicken and cook until lightly browned. When done, set aside to cool.

Beat the eggs in a large bowl, add the spices and cream and whisk until combined. Mix in the chicken and zucchini and pour over the crust.

Bake in the preheated oven for about 30-40 minutes.

When done, allow to cool slightly, slice and serve.

Lunch: Tuna Salad

Servings: 1
Calories: 626, Total Fat: 49.7 g, Saturated Fat: 8.8 g, Carbs: 5.4 g, Sugars: 0 g, Protein: 41.4 g

1 small head lettuce
5 oz tinned tuna, drained and shredded
2 eggs, hard-boiled and sliced

1 medium spring onion, chopped
1 tbsp fresh lemon juice
1 tbsp olive oil
Salt, to taste

Arrange the lettuce leaves on the bottom of a bowl. top with the tuna and eggs. Sprinkle with the onion, drizzle with the juice and olive oil and serve.

Dinner: Roasted Brussels

Servings: 1
Calories: 278, Total Fat: 21 g, Saturated Fat: 9.3 g, Carbs: 4 g, Sugars: 0 g, Protein: 15 g

1 lb Brussels sprouts, ends chopped off
2 tbsp olive oil

Salt, to taste
Black pepper, to taste
8 strips bacon, chopped

Preheat your oven to 375F / 190C. Grease a baking tray and set aside.
Halve the Brussels sprouts, place them in a bowl, drizzle with the oil and season. Toss to coat and transfer to the prepared tray.
Bake in the preheated oven for half an hour, tossing halfway through.
When roasted, transfer to a serving bowl, sprinkle with the bacon and serve.

Day 4:

Breakfast: Vanilla Smoothie

Servings: 1

Calories: 650, Total Fat: 64 g, Saturated Fat: 17.8 g, Carbs: 4 g, Sugars: 1.4 g, Protein: 12 g

---

2 large egg yolks
1/4 cup water
1/2 cup mascarpone cheese
4 ice cubes

1/2 tsp pure vanilla extract
1 tbsp coconut oil
1 tbsp powdered erythritol

Add the ingredients to your blender and blend until smooth.
Pour into a glass and serve.

Lunch: Bacon Veggie Noodle Salad

Servings: 2
Calories: 207, Total Fat: 10.6 g, Saturated Fat: 6.8 g, Carbs: 9.5 g, Sugars: 4.2 g, Protein: 16.1 g

1 cup fresh spinach
4 cups zucchini noodles
1/3 cup crumbled blue cheese

1/3 cup thick blue cheese dressing
1/2 cup crumbled bacon
Black pepper, to taste

Add the ingredients to a bowl, toss to combine and serve.

Dinner: Stromboli

Servings: 8

Calories: 329, Total Fat: 25.6 g, Saturated Fat: 8.4 g, Carbs: 6.3 g, Sugars: 0.2 g, Protein: 18.9 g

---

INGREDIENTS FOR THE DOUGH:
1/4 cup coconut flour
1/2 cup almond flour
1/2 tsp garlic powder
2 tsp baking powder
1/4 tsp salt
1 1/2 cups shredded mozzarella cheese
5 tbsp butter, melted
1 large egg

INGREDIENTS FOR THE STROMBOLI:
12 oz corned beef, chopped
4 oz thinly sliced Swiss cheese
2 tsp caraway seeds

INGREDIENTS FOR THE DRESSING:
1/3 cup mayonnaise
1 tbsp tomato paste
2 tbsp finely diced dill pickle
1/4 tsp ground cumin
2 tsp Swerve Sweetener
1/8 tsp ground cloves

To prepare the dough:
Mix together the coconut and almond flour, garlic powder, baking powder, and salt.
Add the cheese to a saucepan and melt over low heat. Add the egg and butter and mix well until combined. Stir in the flour mixture and transfer to your working surface lined with parchment paper. Knead for a few minutes and set aside.

To prepare the stromboli:
Preheat your oven to 350F / 176C. Grease a baking tray and set aside.
Cover the dough with another piece of parchment paper and roll out into a rectangle. Cut diagonal strips on the long sides of the rectangle.
Spread the beef along the middle of the rectangle and top with the cheese.

Fold the strips of the dough over the beef filling making sure that the ends of the dough overlap. To seal the ends, pinch the dough and sprinkle with the caraway seeds. Transfer to the prepared baking tray and bake in the oven for 25-30 minutes. When done, allow to cool for 15-20 minutes before slicing.

To prepare the dressing:
Mix together the ingredients and serve with the stromboli.

Day 5:

Breakfast: Stuffed Tomatoes

Servings: 2

Calories: 186, Total Fat: 10 g, Saturated Fat: 2.7 g, Carbs: 6 g, Sugars: 0.2 g, Protein: 14 g

2 fresh tomatoes
2 eggs
1 tsp fresh parsley

Salt, to taste
Black pepper, to taste

Preheat your oven to 350F / 176C. Line a baking sheet with parchment paper and set aside.
Chop off the tomato tops and spoon out the seeds.
Arrange the tomatoes onto the prepared the sheet and crack an egg into each tomato.
Bake in the preheated oven for about half an hour.
Allow to cool for a couple of minutes, sprinkle with the parsley, season with salt and pepper and serve.

Lunch: Lemony Rosemary Chicken

Servings: 2

Calories: 209, Total Fat: 10.9 g, Saturated Fat: 1.9 g, Carbs: 0.5 g, Sugars: 0 g, Protein: 9.3 g

1.5 lb chicken tenderloins
1/2 tbsp lemon pepper seasoning
A few sprigs of fresh thyme
1/2 tbsp garlic salt

1/2 tbsp olive oil
10 6-inch rosemary skewers, soaked
in water for up to 3 hours

Preheat your oven to 350F / 176C.
Place the chicken in a bowl, add the remaining ingredients and toss to coat.
Thread each tenderloin on a skewer and arrange in a baking dish.
Bake in the preheated oven for about 40 minutes.
Serve warm.

Dinner: Pizza Peppers

Servings: 4

Calories: 480 Total Fat: 33.7 g, Saturated Fat: 19.1 g, Carbs: 8.4 g, Sugars: 4.5 g, Protein: 32.3 g

4 bell peppers, halved and trimmed
1 lb ground Italian sausage
2 tsp minced garlic
½ large onion, chopped
8 oz sliced mushrooms
14 oz pizza sauce

½ tbsp Italian seasoning
Salt, to taste
Black pepper, to taste
3.5 oz pepperoni, divided use
2 oz sliced black olives
1 cup shredded mozzarella

Preheat your oven to 325F / 160C.
Arrange the peppers in a baking dish and bake in the preheated oven for 20 minutes.
In the meantime, brown the sausage in a skillet on medium-high. Discard the liquid, add the garlic, onion, mushrooms and cook until tender.
Add the sauce and seasonings, mix well and continue cooking on medium-low. When it begins to simmer, stir in half the pepperoni and olives.
Fill the peppers with the mixture, sprinkle with the cheese and the remaining pepperoni.
Bake for a few more minutes until the cheese has melted. Serve warm.

Day 6:

Breakfast: Shrimp Breakfast Skillet

Servings: 4

Calories: 340, Total Fat: 29 g, Saturated Fat: 9.1 g, Carbs: 3.5 g, Sugars: 0.1 g, Protein: 17 g

4 slices uncured bacon, chopped
1 cup sliced mushrooms
4 oz smoked salmon, sliced into strips

4 oz raw shelled shrimp
A pinch Celtic sea salt
Black pepper, to taste
½ cup coconut cream

Heat a skillet on medium, add the bacon and fry for about 5 minutes. Add the mushrooms and sauté for about 5 minutes.

Stir in the salmon and cook for 2 more minutes. Add the shrimp and cook on high for 2-3 more minutes.

Season with salt and pepper, add the cream, reduce the heat to medium-low and cook for 1-2 more minutes.

Serve warm.

Lunch: Pork Tacos

Servings: 4

Calories: 860, Total Fat: 58 g, Saturated Fat: 17.5 g, Carbs: 16 g, Sugars: 0.2 g, Protein: 57 g

INGREDIENTS FOR THE MEAT:
1 tsp ground chipotle pepper
1 tsp cumin
1 tsp cinnamon
2 tsp garlic powder
1 tbsp salt
1 tsp pepper
4 lb pork shoulder
INGREDIENTS FOR THE BROTH:
4 garlic cloves, chopped

1 white onion, chopped
2 tbsp apple cider vinegar
1 cup chicken broth
INGREDIENTS FOR THE ASSEMBLY:
8 low carb wraps
1 cup shredded cheese
1/2 cup mashed avocado
A handful of cilantro
1 cup sour cream

To prepare the pork:
Pat dry the pork, score it and set aside.
Mix together the seasonings, sprinkle them over the pork, rub gently and set aside.
To prepare the broth:
Add the ingredients for the broth to your slow cooker.
Add the pork and press gently. Cover, set on low and cook for about 8 to 10 hours.
When the cooking time is over, transfer the pork into a bowl and shred it.
Drain the cooking liquid but reserve the garlic and onion. Add to the shredded pork and combine.
To assemble:
Spread a layer of the shredded pork over the tacos. Top them with the cheese, avocado, cilantro, and sour cream. Drizzle with the sauce, wrap and serve.

Dinner: Kale Casserole

Servings: 4

Calories: 471, Total Fat: 35 g, Saturated Fat: 12 g, Carbs: 8 g, Sugars: 4 g, Protein: 30 g

2 tbsp olive oil
1 lb lean ground beef
1 tsp onion powder
1 tsp garlic powder
1 tsp oregano

1 tsp kosher salt
½ tsp black pepper
10 oz fresh kale
2 cups marinara sauce
4 oz shredded mozzarella

Heat your broiler on high.

Heat the oil in a Dutch oven on medium-high. Add the beef and cook until browned. Mix in the seasonings and start adding the kale in batches. Continue cooking until the kale has become wilted.

Pour in the sauce and cook for 2 more minutes. Mix in half the cheese and transfer to the Dutch oven.

Top with the remaining cheese and broil for a minute. When the cheese has melted, take out of the oven and leave to rest for a few minutes before serving.

Day 7:

Breakfast: Simple Granola

Servings: 1

Calories: 403, Total Fat: 36.2 g, Saturated Fat: 9.3 g, Carbs: 9.1 g, Sugars: 1.5 g, Protein: 12.6 g

10 whole almonds	**1 tsp chia seeds**
3 Brazil nuts	**1/4 cup pumpkin seeds**
10 cashews	**1 tbsp cacao nibs**
1 tbsp coconut flakes	

Add the ingredients to a bowl, pour in some milk, stir and eat.

Lunch: French Roast Beef

Servings: 8

Calories: 302, Total Fat: 6.3 g, Saturated Fat: 2.2 g, Carbs: 1.1 g, Sugars: 0.2 g, Protein: 56.6 g

1 tsp chopped fresh rosemary
1 tbsp chopped fresh thyme
1 tsp garlic powder

1 tbsp salt
1 tbsp ground black pepper
1 French roast

Combine the spices and rub over the meat. Wrap with several layers of plastic foil and keep in the fridge overnight.

Preheat the oven to 325F / 160C.

Heat a dash of oil in a skillet on medium, add the meat and sear for a minute per side.

Take the skillet off the heat, place in the oven and bake for 10-12 minutes or until the desired doneness.

When done, remove from the oven, transfer to a plate and keep in the fridge for an hour.

Take it out, wrap with plastic foil and allow to rest overnight.

Slice and serve.

Dinner: Egg Roll Bowl

Servings: 6

Calories: 264, Total Fat: 18.6 g, Saturated Fat: 6.4 g, Carbs: 9.4 g, Sugars: 4.5 g, Protein: 15.5 g

1 lb ground pork	1 head of cabbage, thinly sliced
1 tbsp sesame oil	2 tbsp chicken broth
½ medium onion, thinly sliced	Salt, to taste
¼ cup soy sauce	Black pepper, to taste
1 tsp ground ginger	2 stalks of green onion
1 clove garlic, minced	

Add the pork to a wok and brown on medium. Pour in the oil, add the onion and cook until tender and lightly browned.

Meanwhile, whisk together the soy sauce, ginger, and garlic and pour into the wok. Add the cabbage and toss to coat. Pour in the broth and simmer for 3-5 minutes.

Season with salt and pepper, garnish with the green onion and serve.

Day 8:

Breakfast: Jalapeno Frittata

Servings: 4

Calories: 361, Total Fat: 40 g, Saturated Fat: 13.6 g, Carbs: 3 g, Sugars: 1.8 g, Protein: 24 g

---

INGREDIENT FOR THE FILLING:
6 oz cream cheese, softened
2 tbsp salsa verde
2 tbsp chopped jalapeno peppers
¼ cup shredded cheddar cheese
INGREDIENTS FOR THE CUSTARD:
6 eggs
2 tbsp heavy whipping cream

⅓ cup unsweetened almond milk
¼ tsp salt
⅛ tsp black pepper
INGREDIENTS FOR THE TOPPING:
6 slices bacon, cooked and chopped
½ cup grated cheddar cheese
1 tbsp chopped jalapenos

Preheat your oven to 350F / 176C. Grease a 8x8 casserole dish and set aside.

To prepare the filling:

Mix together the ingredients, microwave for a minute, stir well and set aside.

To prepare the custard:

Beat the eggs, add the remaining ingredients and whisk until combined and smooth.

To arrange the frittata:

Spread the filling over the bottom of the prepared casserole dish. Pour the custard over and spread evenly. Top with the ingredients for the topping and bake in the preheated oven for about 35 minutes.

Serve warm.

Lunch: Chipotle Lime Chicken

Servings: 4

Calories: 183, Total Fat: 9 g, Saturated Fat: 2.5 g, Carbs: 2 g, Sugars: 1 g, Protein: 22 g

⅓ cup tomato sauce
3 garlic cloves
2 tbsp olive oil
2 tbsp mild green chilies
3 tbsp lime juice
1 tbsp apple cider vinegar
⅓ cup fresh cilantro

1 tsp ground chipotle powder
1 ½ tsp sweetener of choice
1 tsp sea salt
¼ tsp black pepper
1.5 lb chicken breasts or thighs, bones and skin removed

Add all the ingredients except the chicken to your blender and pulse until creamy and smooth.
Add the chicken to your slow cooker, pour in the sauce and cook on low for 8 hours or on high for 6 hours.
Serve warm.

Dinner: Chicken Enchilada Casserole

Servings: 6

Calories: 447, Total Fat: 28 g, Saturated Fat: 0 g, Carbs: 7 g, Sugars: 0 g, Protein: 43 g

1½ cups enchilada sauce
1 lb chicken breasts, bones and skin removed
Salt, to taste
Black pepper, to taste

4 oz green chiles, chopped
1 cup finely crumbled feta cheese
½ cup minced fresh cilantro
2 cups shredded cheddar cheese

Preheat your oven to 450F / 230C. Grease a casserole dish and set aside.

Pour the sauce into a pan and cook on medium. Pat dry the chicken, season with salt and pepper and add to the pan. Simmer for about 15 minutes, flip and cook covered for 10 more minutes.

When the chicken is cooked through, take it out of the pan, shred it and transfer to a bowl. Add the sauce, chiles, feta cheese, and cilantro and stir to combine.

Spread a cup of the cheese over the bottom of the prepared dish. Top with the chicken mixture and sprinkle with the remaining cheese.

Cover the dish with foil and bake in the preheated oven for 10 minutes. Remove the foil and bake for a few more minutes until the cheese has melted.

Allow to rest for 5 minutes before serving.

Day 9:

Breakfast: Beef, Avocado & Egg Bowl

Servings: 1

Calories: 616, Total Fat: 37.9 g, Saturated Fat: 6.1 g, Carbs: 25.9 g, Sugars: 5.4 g, Protein: 51.5 g

---

Coconut oil
8 mushrooms, sliced
1 small onion, sliced
Salt, to taste
Black pepper, to taste

5 oz ground beef
½ tsp smoked paprika
2 eggs, lightly beaten
10 black olives, pitted and sliced
1 small avocado, diced

Heat some coconut oil in a skillet on medium-high. Add the mushrooms, onions, season with salt and pepper and sauté until soft.

Stir in the beef, sprinkle with the smoked paprika and cook until the beef in browned. Transfer to a plate and set aside.

Add the eggs to the skillet and stir to make scramble eggs. Return the beef to the pan along with the olives and avocado. Cook for a minute, transfer to a bowl, garnish with parsley and serve.

Lunch: Pistachio Cheese Balls

Servings: 2

Calories: 323, Total Fat: 25.6 g, Saturated Fat: 9.9 g, Carbs: 8.1 g, Sugars: 2.9 g, Protein: 16.9 g

1/2 cup pistachios, deshelled and crushed
Salt, to taste

4 oz sundried tomato goat cheese, cut into 7 slices

Add the pistachios to a bowl, season with salt and set aside.
Form each cheese slice into a ball, add to the pistachios and roll to cover each ball with the crushed pistachios.
Serve immediately.

Dinner: Cauliflower Cottage Pie

Servings: 4

Calories: 602, Total Fat: 53.5 g, Saturated Fat: 21.6 g, Carbs: 9.6 g, Sugars: 0.8 g, Protein: 45 g

INGREDIENTS FOR THE MASHED CAULIFLOWER:
1.5 lbs fresh cauliflower, divided into florets
1 tbsp herbal salt
1/3 cup coconut oil
INGREDIENTS FOR THE PORK:

2 lbs ground pork
1/2 white onion, chopped
1 tbsp coconut oil
1-2 tsp salt
1 tbsp mixed spice blend
1/4 cup tomato puree
3.5 oz bacon lardons, fried

To prepare the mashed cauliflower:
Add the cauliflower in a large pot and fill with water. Cook on medium-high for about 20 minutes or until tender.
Strain and discard the water, add the salt and butter and mash the cauliflower until creamy and smooth. Set aside.
To prepare the pork:
Preheat your oven to 350F / 176C.
Melt the coconut oil in a pan on medium, add the onion and sauté until transparent.
Add the pork and cook until browned. Season with the spices, add the tomato puree and stir to combine. Continue cooking on medium for 10 more minutes.
Pour the mixture into a baking dish, top with the mashed cauliflower, sprinkle with the bacon lardons and bake for 30-40 minutes.
Allow to rest for a few minutes before serving.

Day 10:

Breakfast: Salmon-Stuffed Avocado

Servings: 1

Calories: 525, Total Fat: 48 g, Saturated Fat: 11.8 g, Carbs: 4 g, Sugars: 0.1 g, Protein: 19 g

2 oz smoked salmon
2 tbsp olive oil
1 oz soft goat cheese

1 lemon, juiced
A pinch of salt
1 ripe avocado, halved and deseeded

Add the ingredients (except the avocado) to your blender or food processor and pulse until combined.
Fill the avocado halves with the salmon mixture and serve.

Lunch: Chicken Curry

Servings: 4

Calories: 430, Total Fat: 22 g, Saturated Fat: 8.7 g, Carbs: 7 g, Sugars: 0.8 g, Protein: 53 g

INGREDIENTS FOR THE PASTE:
1 cup white onion, chopped
1 oz peanuts, toasted
2 cloves garlic, chopped
3 small red chilies, chopped
1 tbsp water
1 tbsp ginger, grated
2 tsp ground coriander
1 tsp ground cinnamon
1 tsp ground turmeric
1 tsp ground cumin
1/2 tsp black pepper

1 tsp ground fennel seed
INGREDIENTS FOR THE CHICKEN:
2 tbsp olive oil
2 lb chicken thighs, bones and skin removed, chopped into bite-size pieces
3 roma tomatoes, chopped
1 cup chicken stock
14 oz unsweetened coconut milk
1 tbsp lime juice
Salt, to taste
Black pepper, to taste

To prepare the paste:
Add the ingredients to your blender or food processor and pulse until the mixture turns into a smooth paste. Set aside.

To prepare the chicken:
Heat the oil in a wok or pan on high, pour in the paste and cook for about 4 minutes. Stir continuously to prevent burning.

Add the chicken, stir well to coat it with the paste and cook for 2 more minutes.

Stir in the tomatoes, pour in the stock and bring to a simmer. Reduce the heat to low and allow to cook for half an hour.

Pour in the coconut milk and cook for 20 more minutes. stir the curry frequently to prevent burning.

Drizzle with the lime juice, season with salt and pepper, stir and serve warm.

Dinner: Cashew Chicken

Servings: 3

Calories: 333, Total Fat: 24 g, Saturated Fat: 6.4 g, Carbs: 8 g, Sugars: 1.1 g, Protein: 22.6 g

2 tbsp canola oil
3 raw chicken thighs, bones and skin removed, chicken diced
1 tbsp minced garlic
1/4 medium white onion, roughly chopped
1 tbsp green onions
1/2 medium green bell pepper, chopped

1/2 tbsp chili garlic sauce
1/2 tsp ground ginger
Salt, to taste
Black pepper, to taste
1 tbsp rice wine vinegar
1 1/2 tbsp soy sauce
1/4 cup cashews, toasted
1 tbsp sesame seeds

Heat the oil in a pan on high. Add the chicken and cook for 5-7 minutes or until cooked through.

Add the garlic, onions, pepper, sauce, and season with the ginger, pepper, and salt. Cook for 3 more minutes.

Pour in the vinegar and soy sauce and add the cashews. Cook on high until the sauce has thickened.

Transfer to serving bowls, sprinkle with the sesame seeds and serve.

Day 11:

Breakfast: Feta Omelet

Servings: 1

Calories: 570, Total Fat: 46 g, Saturated Fat: 12.6 g, Carbs: 2.5 g, Sugars: 1.5 g, Protein: 30 g

3 eggs	**1 tbsp butter**
1 tbsp heavy cream	**1 tbsp pesto**
Salt, to taste	**1 oz feta cheese**
Black pepper, to taste	

Whisk together the eggs and heavy cream, season with salt and pepper and set aside.
Melt the butter in a frying pan. Pour in the eggs and fry until almost done.
Spread the pesto on top of the omelet and sprinkle the cheese. Fold the omelet in half and let it cook on medium-low for about 5 more minutes.
Serve immediately.

Lunch: Almond Butter Bacon Burger

Servings: 4

Calories: 890, Total Fat: 68 g, Saturated Fat: 18.7 g, Carbs: 8 g, Sugars: 1.6 g, Protein: 54.4 g

INGREDIENTS FOR THE SAUCE:
1 cup water
1 cup almond butter
6 tbsp coconut aminos
4 chili peppers
4 garlic cloves, peeled
1 tbs rice vinegar
1 tsp Swerve

INGREDIENTS FOR THE BURGER:
1.5 lb ground beef
Salt, to taste
Black pepper, to taste
4 slices pepper jack cheese
8 large leaves romaine lettuce
1 red onion, sliced
8 slices uncured bacon, fried

To prepare the sauce:

Pour the water into a saucepan, add the almond butter and bring to a simmer on low. stir frequently to prevent burning.

Stir in the coconut aminos and allow to simmer on low.

Add the remaining ingredients to your blender or food processor and blend until combined and smooth. Transfer to the almond butter and stir well to combine.

Set aside.

To prepare the burgers:

Shape the ground beef into four patties making a small indentation in the middle of each patty.

Arrange in a broiler pan and season with salt and pepper.

Set the broiler on high, and when it's hot enough, place the pan at the mid-high in the oven.

Broil the patties for about 5-7 minutes. Flip and broil for 5-7 more minutes until golden brown on both sides.

Take the patties out of the oven, place the cheese slices on top of the patties and return back to the oven for about 5 more minutes until the cheese has melted.

To assemble the burger:
Arrange two lettuce leaves on each serving dish. Place the patties on top of the lettuce leaves and top with the onion slices.
Spread the sauce on top of the onion slices and garnish with the fried bacon.
Serve immediately.

Dinner: Cauliflower Chowder

Servings: 4

Calories: 237, Total Fat: 18.3 g, Saturated Fat: 4.7 g, Carbs: 6.4 g, Sugars: 3.6 g, Protein: 6.3 g

1 tbsp butter
5 garlic cloves minced
1/2 cup diced onion
1 head of cauliflower, cut into small florets
3/4 cup diced carrots
1 cup milk

1/2 tsp dried oregano
Salt, to taste
1 tsp black pepper
1 cup water
1/4 cup cream cheese
Cooked bacon, for garnishing

Heat the butter in a Dutch oven on high and add the garlic and onion. Sauté until the onions have become soft.

Add the cauliflower, carrots, milk, oregano, and season with salt and pepper. When it begins to boil, reduce the heat to medium and allow to simmer for 15-20 minutes or until the vegetables are tender.

Remove from the heat and blend with an immersion blender. Pour in the water and cream cheese and simmer for 10 more minutes.

Sprinkle with the bacon and serve warm.

Day 12:

Breakfast: Smoothie Bowl

Servings: 4

Calories: 237, Total Fat: 18.3 g, Saturated Fat: 4.7 g, Carbs: 6.4 g, Sugars: 3.6 g, Protein: 6.3 g

INGREDIENTS FOR THE BASE:
1 cup spinach
2 tbsp heavy cream
1/2 cup almond milk
1 tbsp coconut oil
2 ice cubes

INGREDIENTS FOR THE TOPPINGS:
1 tbsp shredded coconut
4 walnuts
4 raspberries
1 tsp chia seeds

To prepare the base:
Add the ingredients to your blender and blend until well combined and smooth. Pour the smoothie into a serving bowl.
Top with the toppings and serve.

Lunch: Steak Salad

Servings: 4

Calories: 451, Total Fat: 26 g, Saturated Fat: 7.4 g, Carbs: 10 g, Sugars: 0.7 g, Protein: 35 g

1.5 lb flat iron steak, sliced into ½-inch slices
1/4 cup balsamic vinegar
3 tbsp avocado oil
6 oz sweet onion, sliced
2 cloves garlic, minced
4 oz cremini mushrooms, sliced
Salt, to taste
Black pepper, to taste

1 head Romaine lettuce, chopped
1 yellow bell pepper, sliced
1 orange bell pepper, sliced
1 avocado, peeled, pitted, and sliced
3 oz sun-dried tomatoes
1 tsp onion powder
1 tsp garlic salt
1 tsp red pepper flakes
1 tsp Italian seasoning

Place the meat into a bowl, drizzle with the vinegar, toss to coat and set aside.
Heat the oil in a pan on medium-low. Add the onions, mushrooms, garlic and season with salt and pepper. Sauté for about 20 minutes or until the veggies are soft and set aside.
In the meantime, combine the lettuce, bell peppers, avocado, and tomatoes.
Arrange the meat in a broiling pan. Mix together the onion powder, garlic salt, red pepper flakes, and Italian seasoning and sprinkle over the meat.
Place the pan on the top rack and broil on high for 5-7 minutes.
To serve, top the salad with the onions and mushrooms and arrange the broiled meat on top.
Serve immediately.

Dinner: Thai Chicken Skewers

Servings: 4

Calories: 319, Total Fat: 24.3 g, Saturated Fat: 3.9 g, Carbs: 7.5 g, Sugars: 3.1 g, Protein: 21 g

INGREDIENTS FOR THE MARINADE:
⅓ cup soy sauce
½ lime, juiced and zested
2 tbsp olive oil
½ tsp garlic
Salt, to taste
Black pepper, to taste
3-4 chicken breasts, cut into strips or chunks

Wooden skewers, soaked in cold water for 30 minutes
INGREDIENTS FOR THE SAUCE:
½ cup spicy Thai peanut butter
1 tbsp soy sauce
4-5 tbsp warm water
¼ tsp garlic powder
½ lime, juiced
1 tsp sriracha

To prepare the marinade and chicken:
Add all the ingredients into a sealable plastic bag. Seal and shake to coat the chicken.
Refrigerate for at least 2 hours.
Preheat your oven at 375F / 190C. Line a baking sheet with foil and set aside.
Thread the marinated chicken onto the soaked skewers and arrange on the baking sheet.
Bake for 15 minutes, flip the skewers and bake for 15-20 more minutes or until the chicken in cooked through.
To prepare the sauce:
Meanwhile, whisk together the ingredients and set aside.
Serve the chicken warm with the sauce as a side.

Day 13:

Breakfast: Cheese Soufflé

Servings: 8

Calories: 288, Total Fat: 23.6 g, Saturated Fat: 12.5 g, Carbs: 3.3 g, Sugars: 0.8 g, Protein: 14.02 g

1/2 cup almond flour
1 tsp ground mustard
1/2 tsp xanthan gum
1/4 tsp cayenne pepper
1 tsp salt
1/2 tsp black pepper
3/4 cup heavy cream

2 cups shredded sharp cheddar cheese
6 large eggs, separated
1/4 cup chopped fresh chives
1/4 tsp cream of tartar
A dash of salt

Preheat your oven to 350F / 176C. Grease 8 ramekins (4 or 6-oz ramekins), arrange on a baking sheet and set aside.

Mix together the flour, mustard, xanthan gum, cayenne, salt, and pepper. Gradually whisk in the cream, cheese, egg yolks, and chives and set aside.

In a separate bowl, beat the egg whites, cream of tartar, and a dash of salt. Gently fold into the egg yolk mixture.

Fill the greased ramekins with the soufflé mixture and bake in the oven for about 20-25 minutes or until the tops of the soufflés are golden brown.

When done, serve immediately.

Lunch: Coconut Chicken Soup

Servings: 4

Calories: 325, Total Fat: 20 g, Saturated Fat: 9.2 g, Carbs: 7 g, Sugars: 0.5 g, Protein: 29 g

6 cups chicken broth	**10 oz mixed mushrooms**
2 stalks lemongrass, chopped and pressed	**1lb chicken thighs, bones and skin removed**
1 inch fresh ginger, grated	**1 tbsp fish sauce**
10 kaffir lime leaves	**1 1/2 cups coconut cream**
1/2 tsp salt	**Cilantro, for garnish**

Pour the broth into a saucepan and heat on medium-high.

Add the lemongrass, ginger, kaffir lime leaves, and salt and simmer for about 20 minutes.

Strain and discard the solids.

Add the mushrooms and chicken to the strained soup and cook on medium for 20 minutes.

Take out the chicken and shred it. Add the shredded chicken back to the soup and stir in the fish sauce and coconut cream.

Cook for 5 more minutes, taste and adjust the seasonings.

Divide the soup into four serving bowls, garnish with cilantro and serve.

Dinner: Bunless Burger

Servings: 2

Calories: 610, Total Fat: 43 g, Saturated Fat: 16.4 g, Carbs: 3 g, Sugars: 0.3 g, Protein: 49 g

4 ground beef patties	**4 lettuce leaves**
½ tsp coarse kosher salt	**2 red onion slices**
½ tsp black pepper	**2 tomato slices**
12 tsp Dijon mustard	**2 slices cheddar**

Heat a skillet, season the patties with salt and pepper and fry them for 2 minutes per side. Transfer to a plate, cover with foil and allow to rest.

To serve, prepare two plates and place a patty on each. Spread a layer of mustard onto each and then layer the lettuce, tomato, onions and top with the cheese and another patty.

Day 14:

Breakfast: Macha Late

Servings: 1

Calories: 148, Total Fat: 15 g, Saturated Fat: 5.6 g, Carbs: 0.5 g, Sugars: 1.3 g, Protein: 1 g

---

1 cup unsweetened cashew milk
1 tsp matcha powder
1 tbsp coconut oil

1/8 teaspoon vanilla bean
2 ice cubes

Add the ingredients to your blender and blend until smooth.
Pour into a glass and serve immediately.

Lunch: Lamb Meatballs & Cauliflower Rice

Servings: 4

Calories: 495, Total Fat: 41 g, Saturated Fat: 19.2 g, Carbs: 3.5 g, Sugars: 0.6 g, Protein: 27 g

INGREDIENTS FOR THE RICE:
7 oz cauliflower florets
Salt, to taste
Black pepper, to taste
INGREDIENTS FOR THE MEATBALLS:
1 lb ground lamb
1 large egg
1 tsp garlic powder
1 tsp paprika
1 tsp fennel seed

1 tsp salt
1 tsp black pepper
OTHER INGREDIENTS:
2 tbsp coconut oil
½ yellow onion, chopped
1 tbsp minced garlic
4 oz goat cheese
1 tbsp lemon zest
1 bunch fresh mint leaves, roughly chopped

To prepare the rice:

Add the cauliflower florets to your food processor and pulse a few times until the cauliflower is coarsely chopped and resembles rice grains.

Heat a dash of oil in a large pan, add the cauliflower rice, cover and cook on medium-low for about 6-8 minutes, season with salt and pepper and set aside.

To prepare the meatballs:

Place lamb in a bowl, add egg and spices and mix by hand to combine the ingredients.

Form about 15 balls and set aside.

Add the coconut oil in a skillet and melt on medium. Add the onion and sauté for about 6-8 minutes or until the onion has become translucent.

Add the garlic and sauté for one more minute or until fragrant.

Place the meatballs on the pan and cook on all sides until they firm.

Divide the cauliflower rice between four plates. Top each portion with meatballs, garnish with the cheese, lemon zest, and mint leaves and serve.

Dinner: Shepherd's Pie

Servings: 6

Calories: 469, Total Fat: 39 g, Saturated Fat: 14.1 g, Carbs: 6 g, Sugars: 0.4 g, Protein: 23 g

1/4 cup oil	1 cup heavy cream
1 lb ground turkey	24 oz riced cauliflower, cooked and drained
3 cloves garlic, minced	
1/4 cup yellow onion, chopped	1/4 cup grated parmesan
1/2 cup celery, chopped	1 cup shredded cheese
1 cup chopped tomatoes	1 tsp dried thyme

Heat the oil in a skillet and add the meat, garlic, onions, and celery. Sauté until the veggies are tender and the meat is browned.

Remove from the heat and mix in the tomatoes. Pour the mixture into a casserole dish and set aside.

Preheat your oven to 350F / 176C.

Add the remaining ingredients to your blender or food processor and pulse until smooth and creamy.

Pour over the meat in the casserole and bake in the preheated oven for 35-40 minutes.

When done, allow to rest for a few minutes before serving.

Day 15:

Breakfast: Keto Waffles

Servings: 5

Calories: 280, Total Fat: 26 g, Saturated Fat: 13.4 g, Carbs: 4.5 g, Sugars: 1.4 g, Protein: 7 g

5 eggs, separated	**1 tsp baking powder**
3-5 tbsp granulated sweetener of choice	**4.5oz butter, melted**
	1-2 tsp vanilla
4 tbsp coconut flour	**3 tbsp full fat milk**

Beat the egg whites until stiff peaks form and set aside.

In a separate bowl, whisk together the egg yolks, sweetener, coconut flour, and baking powder.

Gradually pour in the melted butter and mix until incorporated and the mixture is smooth.

Mix in the vanilla and milk.

Gently fold in the egg whites making sure that the mixture keeps its fluffiness.

Heat your waffle maker, spread enough of the mixture, press and cook as indicated in the manufacturer's instructions.

Repeat the same with the remaining mixture.

Serve warm.

Lunch: Chicken Quesadilla

Servings: 1 quesadilla

Calories: 654, Total Fat: 43 g, Saturated Fat: 15.8 g, Carbs: 7 g, Sugars: 0.8 g, Protein: 52 g

Olive oil, for frying	**1/4 tsp salt**
2.5 oz chicken breast, chopped and grilled	**1 low-carb wrap**
1/4 tsp garlic powder	**3 oz pepper jack, sliced**
1/4 tsp dried basil	**1 tsp chopped jalapeño**
1/4 tsp crushed red pepper	**1/2 avocado sliced thin**

Heat a dash of oil in frying pan on medium-high. Add the chicken, sprinkle with the spices and grill until the chicken is cooked and golden brown on all sides. Set aside.

Place the wrap in a large pan and heat on medium for 2 minutes. Flip and arrange the cheese slices.

Arrange the grilled chicken, and jalapeno, and avocado on one half of the wrap.

Fold the wrap and press with a spatula to flatten.

Serve warm.

Dinner: Amatriciana Pasta

Servings: 4

Calories: 256, Total Fat: 21 g, Saturated Fat: 8.4 g, Carbs: 5 g, Sugars: 0.7 g, Protein: 12 g

7 oz pancetta
2 cloves garlic
1 cup tomato sauce
1/2 tsp red pepper flakes

3 medium yellow squash, spiralized
Salt, to taste
Black pepper, to taste
1/4 cup grated Parmesan cheese

Place the pancetta in a pan and cook on low until the bacon is evenly cooked.
Add the garlic and continue cooking on low for 5-7 minutes or until the garlic has softened.
Mix in the tomato sauce and pepper flakes and allow to simmer until the sauce has thickened.
Add the zucchini, mix to coat, season with salt and pepper and simmer for 2 more minutes.
Divide into serving bowl, sprinkle with the cheese and serve.

Day 16:

Breakfast: Keto Green Smoothie

Servings: 1

Calories: 375, Total Fat: 25 g, Saturated Fat: 10.4 g, Carbs: 4 g, Sugars: 1.5 g, Protein: 30 g

1 oz spinach
1 1/2 cups almond milk
1.7 oz celery
1.7 oz cucumber

1/7 oz avocado
10 drops liquid stevia
1 tbsp coconut oil
1/2 tsp chia seeds, for garnishing

Add the spinach and milk to your blender and blend until smooth.

Add the remaining ingredients and blend again until smooth and creamy.

Pour into a glass, sprinkle with the chia seeds and serve.

Lunch: Cheese & Spinach Rolls with Apple Slaw

Servings: 16-20 rolls

Calories: 670, Total Fat: 67 g, Saturated Fat: 23.1 g, Carbs: 16 g, Sugars: 1.1 g, Protein: 32 g

INGREDIENTS FOR THE FILLING:
Olive oil, for frying
6 oz spinach
1/4 cup grated parmesan
4 oz cream cheese
A pinch of salt
INGREDIENTS FOR THE CRUST:
2 1/2 cups shredded mozzarella
6 tbsp coconut flour

1/2 cup almond flour
2 large eggs
1/2 tsp salt
INGREDIENTS FOR THE TOPPING:
1 apple, grated
3/4 cup cole slaw salad mix
1/4 cup mayonnaise
1/4 tsp salt

To prepare the filling:
Preheat your oven to 350F / 176C. Grease a baking sheet, line with parchment paper and set aside.
Heat a dash of olive oil in a large pan on medium-high. Add the spinach and cook for a few minutes until the spinach has become wilted.
Add the parmesan and cream cheese and stir well to combine. When the cheese has melted, remove from the heat and set aside.

To prepare the crust:
Add the mozzarella to a bowl and microwave for half a minute.
Add the coconut and almond flour and mix well to combine. Add the eggs, season with salt and stir well until combined.
Lay parchment paper on your working surface and spread the cheese dough on top of it. top with another piece of parchment paper and roll out until it is 1/8-inch thick.
Cut the dough into rectangles (approx. 3x4 inch size). Spread the spinach filling over on half of each rectangle and roll them up.
Arrange the rolls on the prepared baking sheet and bake for about 15-20 minutes until the rolls are golden brown.

When done, remove from the oven and allow to cool for about 10 minutes.

To prepare the apple slaw:

Add the ingredients to a large bowl and mix well until combined. Keep in the fridge until serving.

To serve, arrange the rolls on a serving plate and top with the apple slaw.

Dinner: Peanut Chicken

Servings: 4

Calories: 267, Total Fat: 12 g, Saturated Fat: 5.1 g, Carbs: 7 g, Sugars: 0.3 g, Protein: 30 g

1 tbsp olive oil
2 cloves garlic, minced
1 white onion, chopped
16 oz chicken thighs, bones and skin removed
1 large egg

2 large zucchini, spiralized
1/2 tsp chili flakes, optional
1 lime, juiced
2 tbsp soy sauce
1 oz peanuts

Heat the oil in a wok, add the onion and sauté until translucent. Add the garlic and cook for 1-2 minutes until fragrant.

Season the chicken with salt and pepper, add to the wok and cook for about 7 more minutes until it is cooked through. When the chicken is cooked, take it out of the wok, shred and set aside.

Move the onion and garlic to the sides of the wok and crack an egg in the middle. Let it cook for a few seconds and then scramble it.

Add the zucchini noodle and cook for 2 more minutes. Toss while cooking to coat the noodles.

Add the shredded chicken, sprinkle with the chili flakes and drizzle with the lime juice and soy sauce. Toss to combine and divide into serving bowls.

Garnish with the peanuts and serve.

Day 17:

Breakfast: Coconut & Blueberry Porridge

Servings: 2

Calories: 405, Total Fat: 34 g, Saturated Fat: 12.5 g, Carbs: 8 g, Sugars: 0.9 g, Protein: 10 g

---

INGREDIENTS FOR THE PORRIDGE:
1 cup almond milk
1/4 cup coconut flour
1/4 cup ground flaxseed
1 tsp cinnamon
A pinch of salt

1 tsp vanilla extract
10 drops liquid stevia
INGREDIENTS FOR THE TOPPINGS:
1 oz shaved coconut
2 tbsp pumpkin seeds
1/2 cup blueberries

Pour the milk in a saucepan and heat on low.
Add the coconut flour, flax seeds, cinnamon, and salt and whisk to combine and break lumps.
Cook on low-medium and when the mixture starts bubbling, mix in the vanilla and stevia.
When the porridge reaches the desired thickness, remove from heat and pour into serving bowls.
Top with the coconut, pumpkin seeds, and blueberries and serve.

Lunch: Chipotle Steak Bowl

Servings: 4

Calories: 620, Total Fat: 50 g, Saturated Fat: 23.1 g, Carbs: 5.5 g, Sugars: 0.9 g, Protein: 33 g

16 oz skirt steak
Salt, to taste
Black pepper, to taste
4 oz pepper jack cheese, grated
A handful of fresh cilantro
INGREDIENTS FOR GUACAMOLE:
2 avocados, mashed
6 grape tomatoes, diced

1/4 cup red onion, diced
1 tbsp olive oil
1 clove garlic, mashed
1 lime, juiced
Fresh cilantro
1/8 tsp crushed red pepper
1/4 tsp salt
1/8 tsp black pepper

Sprinkle the steak with salt and pepper and set aside.

Heat a skillet on high, add the steak and cook for about 4 minutes. Flip and cook on the other side for 3-4 more minutes.

Transfer to a plate and set aside.

To prepare the guacamole:

Combine the mashed avocados, tomatoes, onions, olive oil, and garlic.

Drizzle with the lime juice, sprinkle with the cilantro and stir well to combine.

Season with crushed red pepper, salt, and pepper and set aside.

To serve:

Cut the steak into thin slices and divide between four plates.

Top with grated cheese and guacamole. Garnish with cilantro and serve.

Dinner: Steak Kebabs

Servings: 6

Calories: 219, Total Fat: 13 g, Saturated Fat: 0 g, Carbs: 5.5 g, Sugars: 0 g, Protein: 20 g

INGREDIENTS FOR THE SAUCE:
2 tbsp olive oil
2 tbsp apple cider vinegar
2 tbsp red onion, finely chopped
1/4 tsp kosher salt
2 packed tbsp parsley, finely chopped
1 clove garlic, minced
2 packed tbsp chopped cilantro
1 tbsp water
1/8 tsp crushed red pepper flakes

1/8 tsp fresh black pepper
INGREDIENTS FOR THE SKEWERS:
1.5 lbs beef, cut into 1-inch cubes
1 1/4 tsp kosher salt
Black pepper, to taste
18 cherry tomatoes
1 large red onion, cut into large chunks
6 bamboo skewers, soaked in water for 1 hour

To prepare the sauce;
Whisk together the olive oil, and vinegar. Mix in the red onion and salt and allow to rest for 5 minutes.
Mix in the remaining ingredients and keep in the fridge until the skewers are ready.
To prepare the skewers:
Season the beef with salt and pepper. Thread the beef together the tomatoes and onions onto the skewers.
Set your grill on high and grill the skewers until the desired doneness rotating from time to time so that the meet is evenly cooked.
When done, transfer to a serving plate, drizzle with the sauce and serve.

Day 18:

Breakfast: California-Style Chicken Omelet

Servings: 1

Calories: 415, Total Fat: 32 g, Saturated Fat: 15.7 g, Carbs: 4 g, Sugars: 0.3 g, Protein: 25 g

---

INGREDIENTS:
2 eggs
Salt, to taste
Black pepper, to taste
1 oz deli cut chicken
1/4 avocado, sliced
2 slices bacon, cooked and chopped
1 campari tomato, sliced
1 tbsp mayonnaise
1 tsp mustard

Beat the eggs and set aside.
Heat a pan and pour the eggs. Season with salt and pepper and cook for about 5 minutes.
When the eggs are almost cooked, top one half of the omelet with the chicken, avocado, bacon, and tomato. Spread the mayo and mustard on top.
Fold the omelet, cover the pan and cook for 5 more minutes.
Serve warm.

Lunch: Caveman Pizza

Servings: 6 portions

Calories: 451, Total Fat: 31.6 g, Saturated Fat: 16.2 g, Carbs: 4.5 g, Sugars: 1 g, Protein: 15 g

INGREDIENTS FOR THE CRUST:
1 medium cauliflower, divided into florets
1 cup chia seeds, ground
1 cup water
3 tbsp olive oil
1 tsp Celtic sea salt
INGREDIENTS FOR TOPPING 1:
½ cup grated parmesan cheese
½ cup heavy cream
½ cup cream cheese
2 cloves garlic, peeled
INGREDIENTS FOR TOPPING 2:
1 cup tomato puree
1 cup sliced cherry tomatoes
1 cup sliced mushrooms
½ cup sliced kalamata olives

To prepare the crust:
Add the cauliflower to your food processor and pulse until finely chopped.
Add the ground chia seeds, pour in water and olive oil, season with salt and pulse until the mixture turns into dough. Transfer to a bowl and leave to rest for 20 minutes.
Preheat you oven to 100F / 37C. Grease a baking sheet and set aside.
Transfer the dough to the prepared baking sheet, press to spread until it is ½-inch thick.
Bake in the preheated oven for about an hour. When the crust is dry and cooked, remove from the oven and turn up the temperature to 400F / 200C.
To prepare topping 1:
Pulse all ingredients in food processor until combined. Spread over one half of the crust.
To prepare topping 2:
Spread the tomato puree over the other half of the crust.
Top with the remaining ingredients and bake for 10 minutes. Slice and serve warm.

Dinner: Cabbage Lasagna

Servings: 2 slices

Calories: 451, Total Fat: 34 g, Saturated Fat: 17 g, Carbs: 9 g, Sugars: 3 g, Protein: 27 g

1 head cabbage, outer leaves removed
3 large eggs
1 1/2 cups grated parmesan cheese
3 lbs ricotta cheese

1/4 cup dried parsley
40 oz marinara sauce
32 oz mozzarella cheese, shredded
2 lbs ground meat, browned
1/4 cup parmesan grated, for topping

Preheat your oven to 350F / 176C.

Carefully separate all the cabbage leaves and add them to a large pot with boiling water. Boil for 5-10 minutes until the leaves have slightly wilted. Drain the water and set the cabbage leaves aside.

Combine the eggs, parmesan, ricotta, and parsley and set aside.

Pour ¾ cup of the marinara sauce into a baking dish and spread it evenly. Arrange a layer of the wilted cabbage leaves and top with half the meat and cheese mixture.

Spread half of the remaining marinara sauce and sprinkle with half the mozzarella. Repeat the layers once again and top with the parmesan.

Bake in the preheated oven for 20-25 minutes. When done, allow to rest for a few minutes before serving.

Day 19:

Breakfast: Raspberry Crepes

Servings: 2

Calories: 285, Total Fat: 20 g, Saturated Fat: 8.1 g, Carbs: 4 g, Sugars: 3 g, Protein: 7.5 g

---

INGREDIENTS FOR THE CREPES:
2 eggs
2 oz cream cheese
2 tbsp erythritol
A dash of cinnamon

A pinch of salt
INGREDIENTS FOR THE FILLING:
½ cup + 2 tbsp ricotta
3 oz raspberries, fresh or frozen

To prepare the crepes:
Add the ingredients to your blender and blend until smooth.
Grease a pan and heat on medium-high. Pour ¼ cup of the batter, swirl to spread it over the bottom of the pan and fry for a few minutes until golden. Flip and fry on the other side as well. Repeat with the remaining batter.
When the crepes have slightly cooled down. Spread about 2 tablespoons of the cheese on top of each. Top with the raspberries, fold and serve.

Lunch: Mackerel Salad

Servings: 2 slices

Calories: 609, Total Fat: 49.9 g, Saturated Fat: 12.5 g, Carbs: 16.1 g, Sugars: 0.5 g, Protein: 27.3 g

INGREDIENTS FOR THE FISH:
2 mackerel fillets
¼ tsp salt
Black pepper, to taste
1 tbsp ghee
INGREDIENTS FOR THE DRESSING:
1 tsp Dijon mustard

2 tbsp olive oil
2 tbsp lemon juice
INGREDIENTS FOR SERVING:
4 cups mixed lettuce
2 cups green beans, boiled
2 large eggs, boiled and quartered
1 medium avocado, sliced

Make diagonal slits on the skin side of the fish. Sprinkle with salt and pepper on both sides and set aside.

Grease a pan with the ghee and het on medium-high. Place the fish skin side down in the pan and fry for a few minutes until the skin is crispy and the fish is cooked.

Remove from the heat, slice and set aside.

To prepare the dressing:

Whisk together the ingredients and set aside.

Place the lettuce in a large bowl, top with the green beans, boiled eggs, avocado, and sliced fish.

Drizzle with the dressing, toss and serve.

Dinner: Chili Chicken

Servings: 4

Calories: 297, Total Fat: 12.2 g, Saturated Fat: 2.7 g, Carbs: 0.5 g, Sugars: 0 g, Protein: 44.2 g

2 lbs boneless chicken thighs
1 tbsp olive oil
1 tbsp chili powder

Salt, to taste
Black pepper, to taste
Lime wedges, for serving

Preheat your oven to 375F / 190C.
Arrange the chicken thighs on a baking tray. Drizzle with the oil and toss to coat. Season with the chili, salt, and pepper and toss again.
Bake in the preheated oven for 15-20 minutes.
Serve warm with lime wedges.

Day 20:

Breakfast: Mocha Chia Pudding

Servings: 2

Calories: 257, Total Fat: 20.2 g, Saturated Fat: 9.4 g, Carbs: 2.2 g, Sugars: 1.8 g, Protein: 7 g

2 cups water
2 tbsp herbal coffee
1 tbsp vanilla extract

⅓ cup coconut cream
2 tbsp cacao nibs
⅓ cup chia seeds

Pour the water into a saucepan, add the herbal coffee and brew for 15 minutes.
When the liquid is reduced to about 1 cup, strain the coffee and discard the solids.
Mix in the vanilla, coconut cream, cacao nibs, and chia seeds.
Transfer to a serving bowl and place in the fridge for at least half an hour.
Serve chilled.

Lunch: Pork Pie

Servings: 8

Calories: 477, Total Fat: 35 g, Saturated Fat: 12.5 g, Carbs: 5.9 g, Sugars: 1.4 g, Protein: 33.1 g

INGREDIENTS FOR THE CRUST:
2 cups ground pork rinds
2 large eggs
¼ cup flaxmeal
1 cup almond flour
½ tsp salt

INGREDIENTS FOR THE FILLING:
2 tbsp ghee
1 medium red onion, finely chopped
2 cloves garlic, crushed
6 large slices bacon, unsmoked
12.5 oz pork loin, diced
4 large eggs
½ cup cream cheese
¼ cup freshly chopped chives
1 cup grated cheddar cheese
½ tsp salt
Black pepper, to taste

To prepare the crust:
Preheat your oven to 400F / 200C.
Add the pork rinds to your food processor or blender and pulse until ground.
Transfer to a bowl, add the remaining ingredients and mix well until dough is formed. Press the dough into a tart pan to spread it evenly.
Top the crust with a piece of parchment paper and add some ceramic baking beans on top. This will prevent the dough from rising. Bake in the preheated oven for about 10-15 minutes. When done, remove from the oven and set aside.

To prepare the filling:
Grease a pan with the ghee and heat on medium high. Add the onion and garlic and sauté for about 7 minutes or until translucent.
Add the bacon and cook for 5 more minutes. Mix in the pork loin and cook on medium until the pork is browned on all sides. Remove from the heat and leave aside to cool.

Preheat the oven again to 400F / 200C.

Beat the eggs and cream cheese. Season with salt and pepper, add the cheese and chives and mix well to combine.

Spread the pork and bacon mixture on top of the crust and pour the egg and cheese mixture.

Bake in the oven for about 20-25 minutes. when cooked, allow to rest for a few minutes.

Slice and serve.

Dinner: Broccoli Beef

Servings: 1

Calories: 688, Total Fat: 37.8 g, Saturated Fat: 21.4 g, Carbs: 8.2 g, Sugars: 0.2 g, Protein: 61.2 g

2 tbsp coconut oil
2 cups broccoli florets
1/2 lb beef, sliced thin and precooked

1 tsp grated ginger
3 cloves garlic, crushed
2 tbsp tamari sauce

Melt the coconut oil in a skillet on medium. Add the broccoli and cook until softened. Add the beef and cook for 2 more minutes. Mix in the ginger, garlic, and tamari sauce. Toss to combine and serve.

Day 21:

Breakfast: Baked Sea Bass

Servings: 2

Calories: 380, Total Fat: 25.9 g, Saturated Fat: 10.4 g, Carbs: 3.4 g, Sugars: 0.8 g, Protein: 27.5 g

10 oz whole sea bass, cleaned and scaled
3 tbsp olive oil, divided use
Salt, to taste
Black pepper, to taste
2 small lemon, 1 sliced, 1 juiced and zested

1/3 cup fresh mint, finely chopped
1/3 cup flat-leaf parsley, finely chopped
1 cup finely grated cauliflower
1/3 cup green olives, finely chopped

Preheat your oven to 400F / 200C and line a baking dish with parchment paper.
Place the bass in the baking dish, drizzle with half the oil and season with salt and pepper.
Stuff the bass with the herbs and half the lemon slices. Bake in the preheated oven for 10-15 minutes.
In the meantime, mix together the remaining ingredients and set aside.
When the bass is done, serve it with the cauliflower salad.

\

Lunch: Halloumi Protein Rolls

Servings: 1

Calories: 410, Total Fat: 36 g, Saturated Fat: 14.9 g, Carbs: 2.9 g, Sugars: 2.4 g, Protein: 17 g

1 tbsp psyllium husk powder
¼ tsp Himalayan pink salt
2 tsp baking powder
5 oz full fat cream cheese
3 large eggs
1 tbsp apple cider vinegar
OTHER INGREDIENTS:

2 knobs butter
1 roll, halved horizontally, toasted
2 leaves lettuce
5 green olives
3 slices Halloumi cheese, grilled
½ tbsp hummus

To prepare the rolls:
Preheat your oven to 400F / 200C. Grease muffin tin and set aside.
Mix together the dry ingredients and set aside.
In another bowl, whisk the wet ingredients and add them to the dry mixture. mix until well combined.
Pour the batter into the muffin tin and bake in the preheated oven for about half an hour.
When done, leave to cool for a few minutes. store in a sealed container at room temperature. The rolls will keep for 4 days.
To serve:
Spread the butter on top of the roll halves. Arrange on the plate with the lettuce, olives, hummus, and cheese and serve.

Dinner: Easy Salmon

Servings: 4

Calories: 402, Total Fat: 14.8 g, Saturated Fat: 2.3 g, Carbs: 0.4 g, Sugars: 0 g, Protein: 63.9 g

1 tsp coriander powder	¼ tsp ginger powder
1 tsp garlic powder	½ tsp salt
1 tsp Kashmiri chili powder	¼ tsp black pepper
2 tsp paprika	3 tsp mustard oil
½ tsp turmeric	1 lb wild-caught salmon
½ tsp garam masala	

Preheat your oven to 425F / 220C. Line a baking sheet with foil and set aside.

Mix together the spices, add the oil and whisk until the mixture turns into a paste. Pour the paste over the salmon and rub to cover the fish.

Arrange the salmon skin side down on the baking sheet and bake in the preheated oven for about 5-10 minutes or the desired doneness.

Serve warm with your favorite salad.

Day 22:

Breakfast: Hemp Heart Porridge

Servings: 1

Calories: 403, Total Fat: 33.2 g, Saturated Fat: 2.5 g, Carbs: 6 g, Sugars: 0.2 g, Protein: 20.7 g

---

INGREDIENTS FOR THE PORRIDGE:
1 cup almond milk
2 tbsp ground flaxseed
½ cup hemp hearts
1 tbsp xyltiol
1 tbsp chia seeds

½ tsp ground cinnamon
¾ tsp vanilla extract
¼ cup crushed almonds
INGREDIENTS FOR TOPPINGS:
1 tbsp hemp hearts
3 Brazil nuts

To prepare the porridge:
Combine the ingredients except the crushed almond to a saucepan.
Cook on medium until it comes to a gentle boil. Give it a good stir and cook for one more minute.
Remove from the heat, mix in the almonds and transfer to a bowl.
Top with the hemp hearts and Brazil nuts and serve.

Lunch: Ham & Cheese Sandwich

Servings: 1

Calories: 774, Total Fat: 65 g, Saturated Fat: 21.7 g, Carbs: 3 g, Sugars: 1.7 g, Protein: 43 g

INGREDIENTS FOR THE BREAD:
1 tbsp psyllium husk powder
¼ tsp Himalayan pink salt
2 tsp baking powder
5 oz full fat cream cheese
3 large eggs

1 tbsp apple cider vinegar
INGREDIENTS FOR THE SANDWICH:
4 slices bread
2 knobs butter
4 slices cheddar
4 slices prosciutto crudo

To prepare the bread:
Preheat your oven to 400F / 200C. Grease a loaf tin and set aside.
Mix together the dry ingredients and set aside.
In another bowl, whisk the wet ingredients and add them to the dry mixture. mix until well combined.
Pour the batter into the tin and bake in the preheated oven for about 35 minutes.
When done, leave to cool for a few minutes. Store in a sealed container at room temperature. The bread will keep for 4 days.
To assemble the sandwich:
Toast the bread slices and spread the butter on one side of each.
Place the cheese and prosciutto on top of two bread slices and top each with the other bread slices.
Serve immediately.

Dinner: Toscana Soup

Servings: 10

Calories: 246, Total Fat: 19 g, Saturated Fat: 7.2 g, Carbs: 7 g, Sugars: 3 g, Protein: 14 g

1 lbs ground Italian sausage	3 garlic cloves, minced
1 tbsp oil	¼ tsp crushed red pepper flakes
½ cup finely diced onion	1 tsp salt
3 cups chopped kale	½ tsp pepper
1 large cauliflower head, diced into small florets	4 ½ cups chicken stock
	½ cup heavy cream

Heat a skillet, add the sausage and cook until browned. Transfer to a slow cooker and set aside. Discard the grease from the skillet and wipe clean it.

Add the oil to the skillet, heat on medium-high, add the onions and sauté for about 5 minutes. transfer the onions to the slow cooker along with the remaining ingredients. Cook on low for 8 hours or on high for 4 hours.

When done, stir in the heavy cream, pour into the serving bowls and serve.

Day 23:

Breakfast: Crunchy Chocolate Cereal

Servings: 1

Calories: 400, Total Fat: 32 g, Saturated Fat: 11.6 g, Carbs: 7 g, Sugars: 1.9 g, Protein: 15 g

---

1/4 cup slivered almonds	**A pinch of Stevia**
1 tbsp chia seeds	**2 tbsp cocoa nibs**
2 tbsp flaxseeds	**Unsweetened almond milk**
1 tbsp shredded coconut	

Mix together all the ingredients except milk.

Pour in the milk, stir and serve.

Lunch: Caprese Salad

Servings: 1

Calories: 528, Total Fat: 45.7 g, Saturated Fat: 16.1 g, Carbs: 2.8 g, Sugars: 1.1 g, Protein: 25.3 g

½ medium tomato, sliced
7 oz buffalo mozzarella, sliced
A splash of white wine vinegar

A drizzle of olive oil
A pinch of Himalayan pink salt
A few basil leaves

Place the tomato and cheese slices in a bowl.
Drizzle with the vinegar and oil, season with salt and toss to combine.
Garnish with basil and serve.

Dinner: Cauliflower & Salmon Medley

Servings: 6

Calories: 232, Total Fat: 14.21 g, Saturated Fat: 8.4 g, Carbs: 5 g, Sugars: 1.6 g, Protein: 17.8 g

2 tbsp olive oil
4 fillets salmon, diced
1 bell pepper, chopped
1 carrot, chopped
2 tbsp shallot, finely diced
2 tbsp sesame oil

4 tbsp soy sauce
2 tbsp Japanese 7-spice
1 cauliflower, riced
Salt, to taste
Black pepper, to taste

Heat the oil in a pot on medium. Add the salmon and sauté for 5 minutes until fried on all sides.

Add the peppers, carrots, and shallot and cook for 5 more minutes.

Pour in the sesame oil and soy sauce, add the seasonings and cook for 3 more minutes.

Mix in the cauliflower rice, turn up the heat to medium-high and give it a good stir.

Season with salt and pepper and serve.

Day 24:

Breakfast: Eggs Benedict

Servings: 2

Calories: 497, Total Fat: 38.1 g, Saturated Fat: 13.8 g, Carbs: 2.4 g, Sugars: 1.3 g, Protein: 30.3 g

INGREDIENTS FOR THE SAUCE:	INGREDIENTS FOR THE EGGS:
2 egg yolks	1 tbsp white vinegar
1 tsp lemon juice	Salt, to taste
2 tbsp butter, melted	4 eggs
1 pinch paprika	4 rolls
1 pich salt	4 slices Canadian bacon, fried
	1 tsp chives

To prepare the sauce:

Whisk the egg yolks in a saucepan and mix in the lemon juice. Heat on very low heat and whisk continuously until the eggs has thickened.

Mix in the melted butter keeping the heat on low. If the heat is not extremely low, the eggs will cook and become scrambled. Alternatively, you can use a double broiler to prepare the sauce.

When done, remove from the heat, sprinkle with the paprika and salt and set aside. If the sauce becomes too thick, mix in a tablespoon of water.

To prepare the eggs:

Fill a pot with water up to 3 inches and bring to the boil. Reduce the heat to a simmer and add the vinegar and salt.

Using a wooden spoon, stir in one direction a few times to create a whirlpool. Gently lower a cracked egg into the whirlpool and leave it to cook for about 5 minutes. Gently take out the egg and place it on a plate lined with a paper towel. Repeat the same with the remaining eggs.

To serve, place an egg on each of the rolls, drizzle with the sauce and sprinkle with the chives, salt, and pepper.

Lunch: Lime Chicken Chowder

Servings: 2

Calories: 692, Total Fat: 49.3 g, Saturated Fat: 24.8 g, Carbs: 5.5 g, Sugars: 4.4 g, Protein: 58.1 g

1 lb chicken thighs, boneless and skinless	**1 lime, juiced**
1 small onion, diced	**8 oz cream cheese**
1 clove garlic, chopped	**1 cup chicken broth**
1 jalapeno, diced	**A few dashes of liquid smoke**
14 oz diced tomatoes	**1 tsp salt**
	1 tbsp pepper

Add the ingredients to your crock pot, set on high and cook for 4 hours or on low for up to 9 hours.

Shred the chicken (without taking it out of the pot) and pour into serving bowls.

Garnish with cheddar cheese, fresh cilantro and serve with lime wedges.

Dinner: Spaghetti Squash Gratin

Servings: 10

Calories: 280, Total Fat: 5 g, Saturated Fat: 0.8 g, Carbs: 8 g, Sugars: 1.4 g, Protein: 5 g

1 large spaghetti squash, cut in half lengthwise, deseeded	2 tbsp butter
2 tbsp olive oil	2 cloves garlic, minced
Salt, to taste	8 slices bacon, fried and crumbled
Black pepper, to taste	¼ cup grated Parmesan cheese
1 onion, thinly sliced	2 cups shredded cheddar cheese
	1 ½ cup sour cream

Preheat your oven to 400F / 200C. Line a baking sheet with foil and set aside.

Place the spaghetti squash on the prepared sheet, drizzle with the oil and season with salt and pepper. Bake for half an hour. When done, allow to cool.

In the meantime, heat a pan on medium and add the onion, butter, garlic, bacon, and season with salt and pepper. Sauté until the onions has browned.

Scoop the squash flesh into a bowl, add the onion and bacon mixture along with the cheese and sour cream. Mix well to combine and pour into a casserole dish.

Reduce the oven temperature to 350F / 176C. Bake the casserole for 20 minutes.

Allow to rest for a few minutes when done before serving.

Day 25:

Breakfast: Shakshuka

Servings: 1

Calories: 490, Total Fat: 34 g, Saturated Fat: 11.9 g, Carbs: 4 g, Sugars: 1 g, Protein: 35 g

1 cup marinara sauce	**1/8 tsp cumin**
1 chili pepper, chopped	**Salt, to taste**
4 eggs	**Black pepper, to taste**
1 oz feta cheese	**Fresh basil, for garnishing**

Preheat your oven to 400F / 200C.

Pour the marinara sauce in a skillet, add the chili and heat on medium. Cook for 5 minutes or until the chili is soft.

Crack the eggs and gently lower them over the sauce. Sprinkle with the cheese and cumin and season with salt and pepper.

Place in the oven and bake for 10 minutes or until the eggs are cooked.

Take it out of the oven, garnish with fresh basil and serve.

Lunch: Herb Salmon Salad

Servings: 4

Calories: 320, Total Fat: 21.5 g, Saturated Fat: 3.8 g, Carbs: 5 g, Sugars: 1.7 g, Protein: 26.4 g

INGREDIENTS FOR THE SALMON:
16 oz salmon fillets
A pinch of Himalayan salt
A dash of ground black pepper
INGREDIENTS FOR THE SALAD:
1 tomato, diced
½ English cucumber, cut in half lengthwise and sliced
2 green onions, finely chopped
4 sticks celery, diced
1 tsp black mustard seeds

¼ cup flat leaf parsley, roughly chopped
INGREDIENTS FOR THE DRESSING:
2 tbsp olive oil
2 tbsp lemon juice
2 tbsp water
2 tbsp Dijon mustard
1 clove garlic
¾ tsp fresh thyme leaves
¾ tsp fresh rosemary leaves
¼ tsp salt
Black pepper, to taste

Turn on your broiler. Line a baking sheet with parchment paper or foil and set aside. Place the salmon on the baking sheet and sprinkle with salt and pepper. broil for 5-10 minutes depending on the thickness of the slices. Once the salmon is browned on top, remove from the oven and allow to cool.

Break the salmon into smaller pieces and place in a bowl. Add the tomato, cucumber, green onions, and celery, toss and set aside.

To prepare the dressing:

Add the ingredients to your food processor or blender, blend until smooth and drizzle over the salad.

Sprinkle with mustard seeds and parsley and serve.

Dinner: Keto Poke with Ahi Tuna

Servings: 2

Calories: 445, Total Fat: 33 g, Saturated Fat: 15.5 g, Carbs: 10 g, Sugars: 1.3 g, Protein: 39 g

8 oz ahi tuna fillet, finely diced
1/2 avocado, diced
1 tbsp coconut aminos
1 tbsp sesame seeds
1/4 red grapefruit, chopped

1/4 cup pili nuts
5 sprigs cilantro, minced
2 tbsp sesame oil
1 tsp sea salt

Add the ingredients to a large bowl and toss to coat.
Divide between serving bowls and serve.

Day 26:

Breakfast: Avocado Chia Smoothie

Servings: 2

Calories: 279, Total Fat: 24.8 g, Saturated Fat: 5.3 g, Carbs: 7 g, Sugars: 3.3 g, Protein: 4.7 g

1–1¼ cups coconut milk
1 tbsp nut butter of choice
½ frozen avocado, grated
1 tbsp chia seeds, soaked in 3 tbsp
water for 10 minutes

1 tbsp coconut oil
2 tsp cacao powder
¼ cup water, if needed
Cacao nibs, for topping
Cinnamon, for topping

Add the ingredients to your blender and blend until creamy and smooth.

Pour into glasses, sprinkle with cinnamon and cacao nibs and serve.

Lunch: Taco Casserole

Servings: 6

Calories: 332, Total Fat: 15.9 g, Saturated Fat: 6.6 g, Carbs: 19.1 g, Sugars: 5.1 g, Protein: 29.5 g

INGREDIENTS FOR THE TORTILLAS:
4 egg whites
11/2 cups unsweetened almond milk
1 tbsp psyllium husk powder
1/2 cup coconut flour

INGREDIENTS FOR THE GUACAMOLE:
1 ripe avocado
1/2 tbsp lime juice
3 tbsp salsa

INGREDIENTS FOR THE CASSEROLE:
1 tbsp olive oil
1 lb ground beef
1/2 cup chopped bell peppers
1/2 onion, chopped
1/3 cup chopped fresh cilantro
1/2 tbsp onion powder
1 tbsp chili powder
1/2 tbsp garlic powder
Salt, to taste
2 cups salsa

To prepare tortillas:

- Whisk the egg white and almond milk. Mix in the psyllium and coconut flour and set aside.
- Grease a skillet with coconut oil, pour in about 4 tablespoons of the batter and fry until golden. Flip and fry in the other side. Repeat with the remaining batter and set aside.

To prepare the casserole:

- Preheat your oven to 350F / 176C.
- Heat the olive oil in a skillet. Add the beef and cook for a few minutes until browned. Add the peppers, onion, cilantro, and spices, stir and cook until the vegetables are tender.

- To assemble the casserole, layer two or more tortillas on the bottom of a casserole dish. Spread a layer of the beef mixture and salsa. Keep layering the tortillas, beef, and salsa until all the materials are used. Bake in the preheated oven for about half an hour. When done, aloe to rest for 10 minutes.

To prepare the guacamole:

- In the meantime, mash the avocado and combine it with the remaining ingredients.
- Slice the casserole and serve with the guacamole.

Dinner: Cheeseburger Casserole

Servings: 6

Calories: 582, Total Fat: 43 g, Saturated Fat: 22 g, Carbs: 2 g, Sugars: 1 g, Protein: 43 g

1/2 lb bacon, diced	1 tbsp yellow mustard
1 lb ground beef	1 tsp seasoned salt
1 clove garlic, finely chopped	4 large eggs
1/2 sweet onion, chopped	1/4 cup heavy cream
2 tbsp reduced-sugar ketchup	1 tsp hot sauce
4 tbsp cream cheese	1 tsp ground pepper
1 tbsp Worcestershire sauce	8 oz grated cheddar

Preheat your oven to 350F / 176C. Grease a casserole dish (approx. 8x8-inch) and set aside.

Heat a skillet on medium and add the bacon. Fry until crisp, transfer to a plate and set aside. Discard the grease and wipe clean the pan.

Add the beef and cook until browned. Drain the grease and add the garlic and onion. Cook for 5 minutes or until the onion has become translucent.

Mix in the ketchup, cream cheese, Worcestershire sauce, and mustard and season with salt. Reduce the heat to low and coon for a few minutes.

Transfer to the prepared baking dish and sprinkle with the bacon.

Beat the eggs, add the heavy cream and whisk until combined. Add the hot sauce and pepper and mix well. Pour the eggs over the beef and bacon and top with the cheese.

Bake in the preheated oven for half an hour. Allow to rest a few minutes before serving.

Day 27:

Breakfast: Blackberry Egg Bake

Servings: 4

Calories: 144, Total Fat: 10 g, Saturated Fat: 2.7 g, Carbs: 2 g, Sugars: 2.1 g, Protein: 8.5 g

5 large eggs	**1 tsp grated fresh ginger**
3 tbsp coconut flour	**1/3 tsp salt**
1 tbsp butter, melted	**1 tsp fresh rosemary**
1/2 orange, zested	**1/2 cup fresh blackberries**
1/4 tsp vanilla	

Preheat your oven to 350F / 176C.

Add the ingredients except the blackberries and rosemary into your blender and blend until creamy and smooth. Add the rosemary and blend for half a minute until the rosemary is chopped and incorporated into the batter.

Pour the batter into four ramekins and top with the blackberries.

Arrange the ramekins on a baking tray and bake in the preheated oven for 15-20 minutes.

Allow to cool for a few minutes before serving.

Lunch: Vietnamese Meatballs

Servings: 4

Calories: 529, Total Fat: 45 g, Saturated Fat: 13.4 g, Carbs: 6 g, Sugars: 3.8 g, Protein: 25 g

INGREDIENTS FOR THE VEGETABLES:
1 medium carrot, spiralized
1 medium daikon radish, spiralized
¼ cup granulated sugar substitute
⅓ cup rice wine vinegar
1 tsp fish sauce

INGREDIENTS FOR THE MEATBALLS:
1lb ground pork
¼ cup almond flour
1 egg
¼ cup scallions, chopped
1 tsp minced ginger

2 tbsp fish sauce
2 tbsp fresh cilantro, chopped
1 tbsp granulated sugar substitute
½ tsp garlic powder
¼ tsp salt

INGREDIENTS FOR THE MAYONNAISE:
1 tbsp granulated sugar substitute
1 tbsp Sriracha hot sauce
½ cup mayonnaise
1 tsp rice wine vinegar

INGREDIENTS FOR GARNISHING:
¼ cup chopped cilantro
¼ cup sliced scallions

To prepare the vegetables:
Place the carrot and radish in a bowl, then whisk together the remaining ingredients, drizzle over the veggies and toss to combine. Keep in the fridge for at least an hour.

To prepare the meatballs:
Add the ingredients to a bowl and mix well to combine.
Form into 16 meatballs and fry in a pan until cooked and golden brown on all sides.

To prepare the mayonnaise:
Whisk together all the ingredients and set aside.

To assemble:
Drain the vegetables and spread them on a serving plate. Arrange the meatballs on top of the veggies and garnish with the scallions and cilantro.
Serve with the mayonnaise.

Dinner: Caprese Hasselback Chicken

Servings: 4

Calories: 365, Total Fat: 21 g, Saturated Fat: 7.8 g, Carbs: 4 g, Sugars: 1 g, Protein: 39 g

4 large chicken breasts	**4 oz mozzarella cheese, sliced**
Salt, to taste	**1/8 cup fresh basil**
Black pepper, to taste	**2 tbsp balsamic vinegar**
2 medium roma tomatoes, thinly sliced	**2 tbsp olive oil**

Preheat your oven to 400F / 200C. Line a baking sheet with foil and set aside.
Make 5 or 6 deep slits into each chicken breast and season on both sides with salt and pepper. Arrange the chicken on the prepared sheet.
Stuff a slice of tomato and mozzarella, and a basil leaf into each slit. Drizzle with the vinegar and oil and bake in the preheated oven for 20-25 minutes.
Serve warm.

Day 28:

Breakfast: Steak & Egg Plate

Servings: 1

Calories: 510, Total Fat: 36 g, Saturated Fat: 12.9 g, Carbs: 3 g, Sugars: 1.4 g, Protein: 44 g

1 tbsp butter	**Black pepper, to taste**
3 eggs	**4 oz sirloin**
Salt, to taste	**1/4 avocado**

Melt the butter in a pan, add the eggs and fry them until the desired doneness. Season with salt and pepper and transfer to a plate. Wipe the pan clean.

Cook the sirloin in a pan until the desired doneness. Slice into strips and arrange on the plate with the eggs.

Add the avocado slices and serve.

Lunch: Smoked Chicken Salad

Servings: 8

Calories: 299, Total Fat: 12.9 g, Saturated Fat: 5.1 g, Carbs: 3 g, Sugars: 0.8 g, Protein: 24 g

1 cup mayonnaise
1 tsp paprika
1 tsp Celtic sea salt

1 green onion, chopped
4 cups cubed, smoked chicken meat

Whisk together the mayonnaise, paprika, and salt.
Mix in the onion and chopped chicken and refrigerate for an hour.
Serve with toasted buns.

Dinner: Spinach Tomato Pizza

Servings: 8

Calories: 344, Total Fat: 14.9 g, Saturated Fat: 7.1 g, Carbs: 4.1 g, Sugars: 1.1 g, Protein: 47.3 g

2 eggs	**2 lbs ground beef**
1/2 cup grated parmesan cheese	**2 tomatoes, sliced**
1 tsp salt	**9 oz frozen spinach, cooked,**
1 tsp garlic powder	**chopped, and drained**
2 tsp Italian seasonings	**2 cups shredded mozzarella cheese**

Preheat your oven to 450F / 220C.

Beat the eggs, add the parmesan, season with salt, garlic, and Italian seasoning and whisk to combine. Add the ground beef and stir to combine.

Pour the mixture into a baking tray and bake for about 20 minutes. When done, drain the grease.

Arrange the tomato slices on top of the beef and egg mixture. layer the spinach and top with the mozzarella.

Bake for a few more minutes until the cheese has melted.

Allow to rest for 5 minutes before resting.

Day 29:

Breakfast: Coconut Pancakes

Servings: 2

Calories: 575, Total Fat: 51 g, Saturated Fat: 20.4 g, Carbs: 3.5 g, Sugars: 4.3 g, Protein: 19 g

2 large eggs	**1/2 tbsp erythritol**
2 oz cream cheese	**1/4 cup unsweetened shredded**
1 tsp cinnamon	**coconut**
1 tbsp almond flour	**2-4 tbsp maple syrup**
1 pinch salt	

Whisk the eggs, add the cream cheese and whisk until incorporated.

Mix in the cinnamon, almond flour, salt, and erythritol.

Grease a pan and heat on medium. Pour in half the batter and cook for about 5 minutes or until browned. Flip gently and cook on the other side until browned.

Transfer to a plate and repeat with the remaining batter.

To serve, sprinkle with the coconuts and drizzle with the syrup.

Lunch: Coleslaw Wraps

Servings: 4

Calories: 609, Total Fat: 50 g, Saturated Fat: 12 g, Carbs: 6.2 g, Sugars: 2.2 g, Protein: 32.7 g

INGREDIENTS FOR THE COLESLAW:
½ cup diced green onions
3 cups thinly sliced red cabbage
2 tsp apple cider vinegar
¾ cup mayonnaise
¼ tsp salt

INGREDIENTS FOR THE WRAPS:
16 collard leaves, stems removed
1 lb ground chicken meat, cooked
and chilled
1/3 cup alfalfa sprouts
Toothpicks

To prepare the coleslaw:
Mix together the ingredients and set aside.
To prepare the wraps:
Remove and discard the stem of each collard leaf. Place a leaf on your working surface and add a spoonful of the coleslaw on the edge of the leaf (opposite of the edge where the stem was sliced off). Add a teaspoon of the meat, top with the sprouts and start rolling the leaf. As you roll, tuck in the sides to keep the wrap sealed. Insert two toothpicks to make sure the leaf won't unroll.
Repeat the same with the remaining leaves and serve.

Dinner: Taco Pie

Servings: 8

Calories: 302, Total Fat: 21.2 g, Saturated Fat: 11.5 g, Carbs: 2.1 g, Sugars: xx g, Protein: 20.2 g

1 lb ground beef	**1 cup heavy cream**
3 tbsp taco seasoning	**1/2 tsp salt**
3/4 cup water	**1/4 tsp black pepper**
6 large eggs	**1 cup shredded Cheddar cheese**
2 cloves garlic, minced	

Preheat your oven to 350F / 176C. Grease a baking dish (approx. 9x9-inch) and set aside.

Heat a skillet on medium-high, add the beef and cook until browned. Sprinkle with the taco seasoning and mix well.

Pour in the water and cook on medium until the sauce has thickened. Transfer to the baking dish and set aside.

Beat the eggs, add the garlic, cream, salt and pepper and mix well. Pour the egg mixture over the beef, top with the cheddar and bake for half an hour.

Allow to rest for a few minutes before serving.

Day 30:

Breakfast: Coconut Pancakes

Servings: 4

Calories: 257, Total Fat: 17.7 g, Saturated Fat: 7.3 g, Carbs: 0.34 g, Sugars: 1.5 g, Protein: 17.6 g

1 lb ground pork	**1 tsp maple extract**
2 tbsp chopped fresh sage	**1 tsp salt**
⅛ tsp cayenne	**½ tsp pepper**
¼ tsp garlic powder	

Add the ingredients to a bowl and mix well to combine.

Form into 8 patties.

Heat a dash of oil in a pan on medium. Add the patties and fry for 3-5 minutes until browned. Flip and fry on the other side for 3-5 more minutes.

Serve immediately.

Lunch: Bacon-Wrapped Chicken

Servings: 8

Calories: 356, Total Fat: 25.5 g, Saturated Fat: 8.3 g, Carbs: 2.3 g, Sugars: 1.3 g, Protein: 27.6 g

2 tsp kosher salt	**1 tsp onion powder**
2 tsp paprika	**1 tsp thyme**
2 tsp cayenne pepper	**2 lbs chicken tenders**
2 tsp garlic powder	**16 slices bacon**
1 tsp oregano	

Preheat your oven to 425F / 220C. Line two baking trays with foil, top with a metal rack and set aside.

Add all the spices and herbs in a plastic bag. Seal and shake to combine.

Place each chicken tender into the bag, seal and shake to coat with the spice and herb mixture.

Wrap each tenderloin with bacon and arrange onto the prepared trays.

Bake in the preheated oven for about 30-35 minutes until the chicken is cooked and bacon crispy.

Serve warm.

Dinner: Mini Pepper Nachos

Servings: 6

Calories: 351, Total Fat: 21.9 g, Saturated Fat: 9.5 g, Carbs: 6.5 g, Sugars: 0.9 g, Protein: 28.4 g

1 tsp ground cumin	1/2 tsp kosher salt
1 tbsp chili powder	1/2 tsp pepper
1 tsp paprika	1 lb ground beef
1/4 tsp red pepper flakes	1 lb mini peppers, halved and seeded
1 tsp garlic powder	1 1/2 cups shredded Cheddar cheese
1/2 tsp oregano	1/2 cup chopped tomato

Mix together the cumin, chili, paprika, red pepper flakes, garlic powder, oregano, salt, and pepper and set aside.

Heat a skillet on medium-high, add the beef and cooked until browned. Add the spice mixture, stir to incorporate and remove from the stove.

Preheat your oven to 400F / 200C. Line a baking tray with foil and arrange the peppers cut-side up. The peppers should stay very close to one another.

Top the peppers with the beef mixture, sprinkle with the cheese and bake in the oven for up to 10 minutes.

When done, sprinkle with the chopped tomatoes and serve.

The "Dirty Dozen" and "Clean 15"

Every year, the Environmental Working Group releases a list of the produce with the most pesticide residue (Dirty Dozen) and a list of the ones with the least chance of having residue (Clean 15). It's based on data from the U.S. Department of Agriculture and reveals that 70% of the 48 types of produce that was tested had residues of at least one type of pesticide. On the thousands of samples, there were 178 different pesticides and pesticide breakdown products. This residue can stay on veggies and fruit even after they are washed and peeled.

All pesticides are toxic to humans, and when there is residue left on our food, it has a negative impact on our health. Consequences can include damage to the nervous system, reproductive system, cancer, a weakened immune system, and more. Women who are pregnant can expose their unborn children to toxins through their diet, and continued exposure to pesticides can affect their development.

This year, pears and potatoes join the Dirty Dozen, while cucumbers and cherry tomatoes were removed. Those two types of produce are not on the Clean 15 list, though, so they're clearly still a risk for pesticide residue. This info can help you choose the best fruits and veggies, as well as which ones you should always try to buy organic.

THE DIRTY DOZEN

Strawberries	*Grapes*
Spinach	*Pears*
Nectarines	*Cherries*
Apples	*Tomatoes*
Peaches	*Sweet bell peppers*
Celery	*Potatoes*

THE CLEAN 15

Sweet corn	*Mangoes*
Avocados	*Eggplant*
Pineapples	*Honeydew*
Cabbage	*Kiwi*
Onions	*Cantaloupe*
Frozen sweet peas	*Cauliflower*
Papayas	*Grapefruit*
Asparagus	

Measurement Conversion Tables

Volume Equivalents (Liquid)

US Standard	US Standard (ounces)	Metric (Approx.)
2 tablespoons	1 fl oz	30 ml
¼ cup	2 fl oz	60 ml
½ cup	4 fl oz	120 ml
1 cup	8 fl oz	240 ml
1 ½ cups	12 fl oz	355 ml
2 cups or 1 pint	16 fl oz	475 ml
4 cups or 1 quart	32 fl oz	1 L
1 gallon	128 fl oz	4 L

Oven Temperatures

Fahrenheit (F)	Celsius (C) (Approx)
250°F	120°C
300°F	150°C
325°F	165°C
350°F	180°C
375°F	190°C
400°F	200°C
425°F	220°C
450°F	230°C

Volume Equivalents (Dry)

US Standard	Metric (Approx.)
¼ teaspoon	1 ml
½ teaspoon	2 ml
1 teaspoon	5 ml
1 tablespoon	15 ml
¼ cup	59 ml
½ cup	118 ml
1 cup	235 ml

Weight Equivalents

US Standard	Metric (Approx.)
½ ounce	15 g
1 ounce	30 g
2 ounces	60 g
4 ounces	115 g
8 ounces	225 g
12 ounces	340 g
16 ounces or 1 pound	455 g

References and Resources

Dashti, Hussein M et al. "Long-Term Effects of a Ketogenic Diet in Obese Patients." *Experimental & Clinical Cardiology* 9.3 (2004): 200–205. Print.

Emmerich, Maria. "Home – Landing Page." *Keto-Adapted*, keto-adapted.com/.

Galgano, F., Favati, F., Caruso, M., Pietrafesa, A. and Natella, S. (2007), The Influence of Processing and Preservation on the Retention of Health-Promoting Compounds in Broccoli. Journal of Food Science, 72: S130–S135. doi:10.1111/j.1750-3841.2006.00258.x

Newman, John C. *Ketogenic Diet Reduces Midlife Mortality and Improves Memory in Aging Mice.* Cell Metabolism, www.cell.com/cell-metabolism/fulltext/S1550-4131(17)30489-8+.

Oey, Indrawati, et al. "Does High Pressure Processing Influence Nutritional Aspects of Plant Based Food Systems?" *Trends in Food Science & Technology*, Elsevier, 23 Sept. 2007, www.sciencedirect.com/science/article/pii/S0924224407002749.

Kosinski, Christophe, and François R Jornayvaz. "Effects of Ketogenic Diets on Cardiovascular Risk Factors: Evidence from Animal and Human Studies." *Nutrients*, vol. 9, no. 517, 2017.

Volek, Jeff S., et al. *The Art and Science of Low Carbohydrate Living: an Expert Guide to Making the Life-Saving Benefits of Carbohydrate Restriction Sustainable and Enjoyable*. Beyond Obesity, 2011.

Volek, Jeff S., and Stephen D. Phinney. *The Art and Science of Low Carbohydrate Performance*. Beyond Obesity LLC, 2012.

Zajac, Adam et al. "The Effects of a Ketogenic Diet on Exercise Metabolism and Physical Performance in Off-Road Cyclists." *Nutrients* 6.7 (2014): 2493–2508. *PMC*. Web. 18 Nov. 2017.

Ziauddin, K.Syed. "Observations on Some Chemical and Physical Characteristics of Buffalo Meat." *Meat Science*, Elsevier, 14 Oct. 2003, www.sciencedirect.com/science/article/pii/0309174094901481

Zinn, Caryn, et al. "Ketogenic Diet Benefits Body Composition and Well-Being but Not Performance in a Pilot Case Study of New Zealand Endurance Athletes." *Journal of the International Society of Sports Nutrition*, BioMed Central, 12 July 2017,
jissn.biomedcentral.com/articles/10.1186/s12970-017-0180-0.

Recipe Index

Made in the USA
Columbia, SC
31 March 2018